Home Security System DIY PRO using Android and TI CC3200 SimpleLink

Robert Chin

Table of Contents

About the Author

Introduction

About the Author:

Robert Chin has a Bachelor of Science degree in computer engineering and is experienced in developing projects on the TI CC3200 SimpleLink, Android, Arduino, and PC Windows platforms using C/C++, Java, Unreal Script, DirectX, OpenGL, and OpenGL ES 2.0. He is the author of "Home Security Systems DIY using Android and Arduino" and "Beginning Arduino ov7670 Camera Development". He is also the author of "Beginning Android 3d Game Development", and "Beginning IOS 3d Unreal Games Development" both published by Apress and was the technical reviewer for "UDK Game Development" published by Course Technology CENGAGE Learning. Beginning Android 3d Game Development was licensed to Tsinghua University through Tsinghua University Press.

Introduction

This book shows you how to build and modify your own wifi camera based commercial quality portable wireless security, surveillance, and spy system appropriate for use at home, or during travel. This system uses only an Android cell phone or tablet(operating system 2.2 and above), a TI CC3200 Launchpad or ArduCAM CC3200 UNO, and a TI Camera Booster Pack or just an ArduCAM MT9D111 digital camera if you are using an ArduCAM CC3200 Uno which has a built in camera interface. I recommend the ArduCAM CC3200 Uno for use with the project in this book because of the built in camera interface and superior layout and design. The Texas Instruments CC3200 microprocessor was selected for this book because it provides high quality built in Wifi capabilities that provide for high quality real time video surveillance and motion detection. This book shows you how to build and modify your own alarm system that detects the motion of an intruder, calls out to an emergency phone number and sends emergency text messages using an Android cell phone or just alerts you to the intruder using an Android tablet. This alarm system is compact enough to also provide portable security for travelers using hotels and motels or you can use this as a hidden spy camera system. You can also use the security system for high quality continuous real time surveillance of your property. The live video feed is shown on the Android device. The camera can be set to only record pictures where there is movement so you can easily view any saved images to determine what kind of intruder was detected. The image data is stored locally on the Android device and does NOT require payment of storage fees as with some home security company plans. This book will also go into the technical details of the hardware set up as well as the author created Android and TI CC3200 SimpleLink software. With these technical details you will be able to customize and expand these systems to suit your specific needs for your own personal use. This book also serves as a quick start guide for people interested in learning how to program wifi communication between an Android and a TI CC3200 Simplelink device.

> Important Note: The official support web site for this book along with direct links to downloadable code and executables are listed in Chapter 8.

A summary of the content of the book's chapters follows.

Chapter 1: Introducing the ArduCAM CC3200 UNO – In this chapter I introduce the ArduCAM CC3200 Uno board which is compatible with the TI CC3200 Launchpad board. I cover the software you will need to install on your computer in order to develop programs on a CC3200 device. I conclude the chapter with a "Hands on Example" where I walk the reader through the compilation and installation of an example program from the standard Texas Instruments CC3200 SDK.

Chapter 2: TI CC3200 SimpleLink Programming Language Basics - In this chapter I cover the C programming language that is used in developing programs for the CC3200 device.

Chapter 3: The Android Controller and Wifi Communication – This chapter covers the software you will need to install in order to develop Android programs. Wifi communication between the Android device and the CC3200 device and the related code is also discussed.

Chapter 4: The CC3200 and Wifi Communication – In this chapter I cover wifi communication using the CC3200 and the associated code that you will need to implement it.

Chapter 5: Motion Detection Using a Camera- This chapter discusses the motion detection method and how it is implemented on the Android device in code.

Chapter 6: The Android Wireless Security System Design – In this chapter I cover the Android side of the security system presented in this book and how it is implemented in code on the Android device.

Chapter 7: The CC3200 Simplelink Wireless Security System Design - This chapter covers the CC3200 device side of the security system presented in this book and the code that implements it.

Chapter 8: Hands on Example: Building an Android and TI CC3200 Simplelink Security System – In this chapter I give the reader a quick start guide to installing and operating the GotchaCAM home security and surveillance system that is presented in this book.

Chapter 9: Deploying your GotchaCAM Wireless Intruder Alarm and Surveillance System – In this chapter I give you some tips and recommendations on how to deploy your new GotchaCAM alarm system.

Chapter 1

Introducing the ArduCAM CC3200 UNO

In this chapter I discuss the ArduCAM CC3200 Uno board which I used to create the software that actually captures the image and then sends it to the Android phone using wifi for processing. I begin by describing the features of the board. I then give installation information about the key programs you will need for developing software on the CC3200 platform. These key programs include TI Code Composer Studio, Uniflash, PinMux, Terra Term, and TI Real Time Operating System. Finally, I present a "Hands on Example", where I take the reader step by step through the installation and testing of a CC3200 Simplelink project. This project will serve as the basis for the CC3200 code for the home security system developed in this book.

What is the TI CC3200 Simplelink

The TI CC3200 Simplelink chip is a wireless MCU (Micro Controller) integrating high-performance ARM® Cortex™-M4 MCU with on-chip Wi-Fi, internet, and robust security protocols. It can be used to develop an entire IoT (Internet of things) application with a single IC.

The official web page for the CC3200 is located at:

http://processors.wiki.ti.com/index.php/CC31xx_%26_CC32xx

The CC3200 is what is used in the TI CC3200 Launchpad board made by Texas Instruments.

Overview of the ArduCAM CC3200 Uno

The ArduCAM CC3200 Uno is a board made by ArduCAM that uses the TI CC3200 Simplelink chip and is compatible with the TI CC3200 Launchpad. It also contains a built in camera interface that is compatible with the CC3200CAMBOOST pack from Texas Instruments. The camera related examples in the CC3200 SDK from Texas instruments designed for the Launchpad with the TI camera booster pack also work with the ArduCAM CC3200 Uno. The ArduCAM board is the same size as the Arduino Uno and it also has the same layout of the pins. I highly recommend you buy this board if you are interested in doing a wifi camera related project using the CC3200.

Key Features of the ArduCAM CC3200 Uno:

-   TI CC3200 ARM Cortex M4 Processor with WIFI support

- Arduino UNO Size and Pin Out

- Supports the ArduCAM Standard Camera Interface and MT9D111 Camera Module

- Onboard JTAG/SWD Debugger

- Supports Energia and Code Composer Studio Development Environment

- ARM Cortex-M4 Core at 80 MHz

- 256KB RAM, 1MB serial flash memory with file system for user

- Hardware Crypto Engine for Advanced Fast Security, Including AES, DES, 3DES, SHA2 MD5, CRC and Checksum

- Up to 27 individually programmable, multiplexed GPIO pins, including a fast parallel camera interface, I2S, SD/MMC, UART, SPI, I2C, and four-channel ADC.

- Dedicated ARM MCU, completely offloads Wi-Fi and Internet Protocols from the Application Microcontroller

- 802.11 b/g/n Radio

- WPA2 Personal and Enterprise Security

- Station, Access Point, and Wi-Fi Direct Modes

- Powerful Crypto Engine for Fast, Secure Wi-Fi and Internet Connections with 256-Bit AES Encryption for TLS and SSL connections

- SmartConfig Technology, AP Mode and WPS2 for easy and flexible Wi-Fi provisioning

- The power-management subsystem includes integrated DC-DC converters supporting a wide range of supply voltages. This subsystem enables low-power consumption modes, such as the hibernate with RTC mode requiring less than 7 µA of current

- Easy to use SDK with full APIs with lots of examples for Energia, GCC,IAR System and Ti Code Composer Studio (CCS)

The documentation for the ArduCAM CC3200 Uno can be found on ArduCAM's web site at:

http://www.arducam.com

A direct link to the official documentation of the ArduCAM CC3200 Uno is available at:

http://www.arducam.com/downloads/CC3200_UNO/ArduCAM_CC3200_UNO_DS.pdf

A picture of the ArduCAM CC3200 Uno that I used in developing and testing the software for this book is in Figure 1-1. The ArduCAM CC3200 Uno can be purchased on Amazon and Ebay for around $40. The ArduCAM MT9D111 camera can be purchased for around $10.00. The MT9D111 camera fits into the camera socket on the ArduCAM CC3200 UNO and is required for this book. The MT9D111 is shown in Figure 1-2.

Figure 1-1. The ArduCAM CC3200 UNO

Figure 1-2. The ArduCAM MT9D111 Camera

10

The Texas Instruments CC3200 Camera Booster Pack

I recommend the ArduCAM CC3200 Uno board for the home security system project developed in this book. However, you should be able to use the standard TI CC3200 Launchpad board from Texas Instruments with the TI CC3200 Camera BoosterPack also. The user manual for the Camera Boosterpack board is called the "CC3200 SimpleLink Wi-Fi® and IoT Solution with MCU Camera BoosterPack User's Guide" and can be downloaded from the link below.

http://www.ti.com/lit/ug/swru384/swru384.pdf

One important thing to note is that you need to make sure that the camera boosterpack board aligns correctly according to the manual otherwise according to the manual "failure to align the boards correctly before power-up can damage the boards."

System Requirements for TI Code Composer Studio

TI Code Composer Studio 6.0.1 or greater is required for use with this book. This is the minimum version of the program that supports the CC3200 chip.

The system requirements for the Code Composer Studio version 6 development environment is:

Memory: 4GB

Disk space: 400MB minimum

Processor: 1.0GHz x86 compatible processor

Windows: XP Service Pack 3, Windows 7 (Service Pack 1 or later) and Windows 8.x is

               supported by all CCSv6 versions. Windows 10 is supported by CCS versions

               6.1.3 and greater

Linux: The CC3200 is not supported by the Linux version of Code Composer Studio.

Mac: MacOS is supported by CCS versions 6.1.3 and greater

> Note: I was able to get Code Composer Studio to work with my Windows XP Service Pack 2 version of the operating system.

Installing the CC3200 SDK and CC3200 SDK Service Pack

The SDK for the CC3200 contains the code project examples and libraries that you will need to install before using the TI Code Composer Studio. The Service Pack for the CC3200 SDK is to be installed on the CC3200 device itself using the Uniflash program. There is a button in the Uniflash program that is used to install the service pack to the device. For more information on the Uniflash program see:

http://processors.wiki.ti.com/index.php/CC3100_%26_CC3200_Serial_Flash_Guide

The web page for the CC3200 SDK download and the CC3200 SDK Service Pack is located at:

http://www.ti.com/tool/cc3200sdk

Installing the TI Code Composer Studio

The minimum version needed is Code Composer Studio 6.0.1 which is the beginning of support for the CC3200. This is the version I used on my Windows XP system for this book. The TI Code Composer Studio can be downloaded at:

http://www.ti.com/tool/ccstudio

The download comes in two forms that are:

- A small executable that installs most of the software components using the internet. This version requires a computer with internet access. If you have a firewall or anti-virus program you may have to turn these off or modify them in order for the installer to work correctly.

- A large executable (around 730 MB) which contains most of the needed components for the project in this book. This can be installed offline without any internet connection. This is how I installed my version of Code Composer Studio that I used with this book.

By default the Code Composer Studio installs a "Free" license. Other licenses are also available.

The web page where you can download the web and offline install versions for the current as well as past versions of Code Composer Studio is located at:

http://processors.wiki.ti.com/index.php/Download_CCS

In terms of installation you can accept the default installation settings for most of the screens. For the "Processor Support" screen you need to select "CC32xx Device Support" and the "TI ARM Compiler". See Figure 1-3.

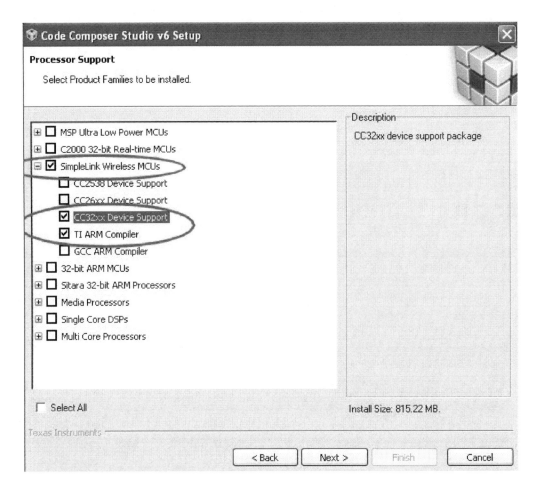

Figure 1-3. The Processor Support Selection Screen

Installing the TI Real Time Operating System Code Composer Studio Component

In order to compile the security system project presented in this book and the examples in the SDK that use the TI Real Time Operating System you will need to install these key components.

The main information page for the TI Real Time Operating System is at:

http://www.ti.com/tool/ti-rtos

The download page is at:

http://www.ti.com/tool/ti-rtos-mcu

After you install this onto your hard drive you will need to start Code Composer Studio to finish the installation. Code Composer Studio should automatically detect that the real time operating system files needs to be installed and it should then install them.

Installing Uniflash

Uniflash is the program that you will use to write or "flash" the program code for the TI CC3200 Simplelink chip onto your CC3200 device.

The Uniflash download web site is at:

http://www.ti.com/tool/uniflash

You can accept most of the default installation settings for this program. The key components to install are for the "SimpleLink WIFI 31XX/32XX". These are selected from the "Select Components" screen. All the other components are optional. See Figure 1-4.

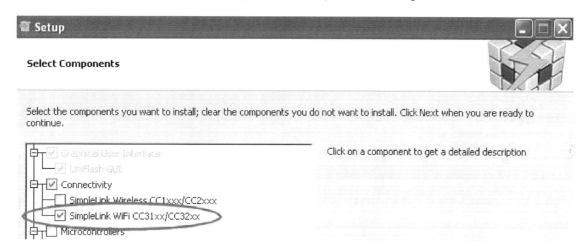

Figure 1-4. Uniflash Select Components

Installing TI PinMux

The TI PinMux tool generates code that maps pins on the CC3200 chip to output pins such as those on the camera adapter.

The download web page is located at:

http://processors.wiki.ti.com/index.php/TI_PinMux_Tool

The important thing about the Pin Mux Tool is that it comes in a cloud version that requires an internet connection and a standalone version which does not. Both versions can be downloaded on the download web page. Also, different versions of the Pin Mux Tool can be downloaded.

Installing Terra Term

Terra Term is a program that allows you to see debug output that is printed to the Terra Term program using the Report() function or the UART_PRINT() function which is actually a macro for the Report() function.

The link to the Terra Term software download is located at:

http://en.sourceforge.jp/projects/ttssh2/releases/

Important Resources

This section covers some of the key resources that you will need to fully understand the CC3200. Documentation for the TI CC3200 Launchpad is dispersed widely and is hard to find in many cases so this section serves as a valuable guide to learning more about the CC3200.

- The CC3200 main web page – This web page is dedicated to the CC3100 and the CC3200 and contains links to vital information concerning the CC3200.

  http://processors.wiki.ti.com/index.php/CC31xx_%26_CC32xx

- CC32XX SimpleLink Host Driver Documentation – This is a web page that is located in the docs/simplelink_api/html directory in the SDK installation. This covers the functions relating to wifi communications.

  file:///C:/TI/CC3200SDK_1.1.0/cc3200-sdk/docs/simplelink_api/html/index.html

- CC3200 Peripheral Driver Library User's Guide – This is an executable help file that is located in the doc directory of the SDK installation. This covers the built in ROM functions that control the CC3200 peripherals such as the camera and camera interface.

C:\TI\CC3200SDK_1.1.0\cc3200-sdk\docs\CC3200-Peripheral_Driver_Library_User's_Guide.chm

- CC3100/CC3200 SimpleLink Wi-Fi® Internet on-a-Chip User's Guide is a pdf file that is located at:

  http://processors.wiki.ti.com/index.php/CC32xx_Programmers_Guide

- CC3200 SimpleLink Wi-Fi® and IoT Solution, a Single Chip Wireless MCU Programmer's Guide is a pdf file that is located at:

http://processors.wiki.ti.com/index.php/CC32xx_Programmers_Guide

- CC3200 Technical Reference Manual is a pdf file that is located at:

  http://processors.wiki.ti.com/index.php/CC32xx_Technical_Reference_Manual

- The ArduCAM specific documentation is located at:

  http://www.arducam.com/downloads/CC3200_UNO/ArduCAM_CC3200_UNO_DS.pdf

- Help from Texas Instruments Engineers – Get help from actual Texas Instruments engineers by posting to the forum located at:

  http://e2e.ti.com/

  A response usually takes around a week and is posted to the forum.

Hands on Example: The Simplelink "Hello World" Project

In this hands on example I guide you through the compilation, installation and testing of the wlan_ap example. This example will serve as the basis for the final program on your CC3200 device that sends images to your Android device for processing.

Install the TI Code Composer Studio and the TI Real Time Operating System

In order to run the wlan_ap project you will need to install the TI Code Composer Studio and the TI Real Time Operating System. Refer to the section regarding the TIRTOS installation information discussed previously in this chapter.

Importing the ti_rtos_config and the wlan_ap projects from the CC3200 SDK

In order to compile the wlan_ap project you will need to import the ti_rtos_config project from the CC3200 SDK. In order to import a project into the current workspace select the Project->Import CSS Projects menu item to begin the process. See Figure 1-5.

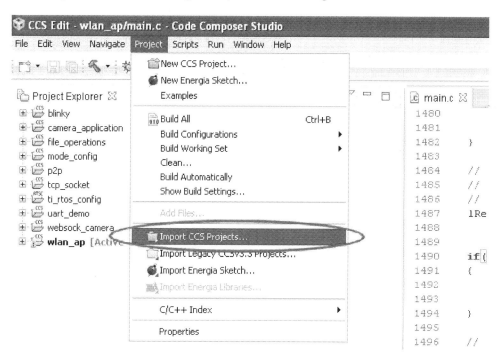

Figure 1-5. Importing a CSS Project into the current workspace

After the wlan_ap project and the ti_rtos_config projects have been imported into the Code Composer Studio's workspace there should be new entries in the "Project Explorer" section of the IDE similar to what is shown in Figure 1-6.

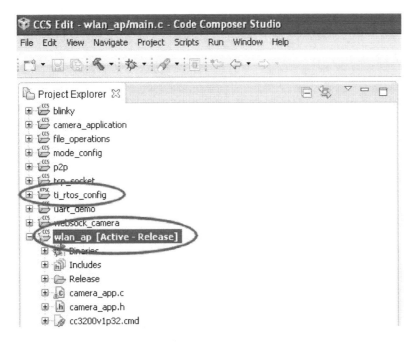

Figure 1-6. The wlan_ap project and the ti_rtos_config project

Building the ti_rtos_config and wlan_ap Projects

Next, the ti_rtos_config and then the wlan_ap projects need to be built. In order to do this you need to select the Project->BuildProject menu item for each project. See Figure 1-7.

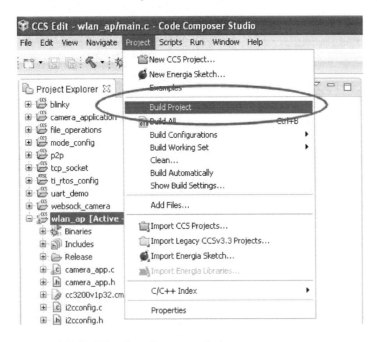

Figure 1-7. Building the wlan_ap project

Writing the wlan_ap binary to the CC3200 device using Uniflash

Next, you need to write a copy of the wlan_ap.bin file which is the binary executable image of the program you just imported and built onto your CC3200 device which in my case was the ArduCAM CC3200 UNO. This section discusses the steps you need to perform in order to write the executable image to the CC3200 device.

Preparing the CC3200 for flashing

In order to write the program file to the device you first need to put a jumper on the SOP2 (Sense On Power Up) group of pins. You also should put jumpers on the FT_RX and FT_TX set of pins. All other jumper pins should be clear. See Figure 1-8.

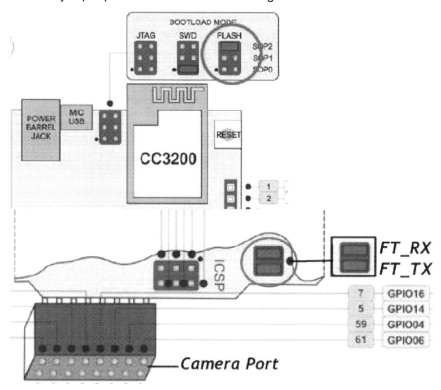

Figure 1-8. Changing the Sense On Power Up jumper for Uniflash for the ArduCAM CC3200 Uno

Plug in the CC3200 device into an available USB port.

Setup New Target Configuration

The first time you start up Uniflash you will need to create a new target configuration by clicking the link "New Target Configuration" under the "Quick Start Guide" section. In the popup window that comes up you will need to specify the type of connection which is the serial uart interface for the CC3200 and the board or device which is Simplelink wifi CC3100/CC3200. See Figure 1-9. You can then save this target configuration if you desire. Saving the session saves the information regarding the interface and device and other session information such as location of the program binary you want to write. In later flashing sessions you can recall this previously saved target configuration to skip the selection of the interface, device, etc.

18

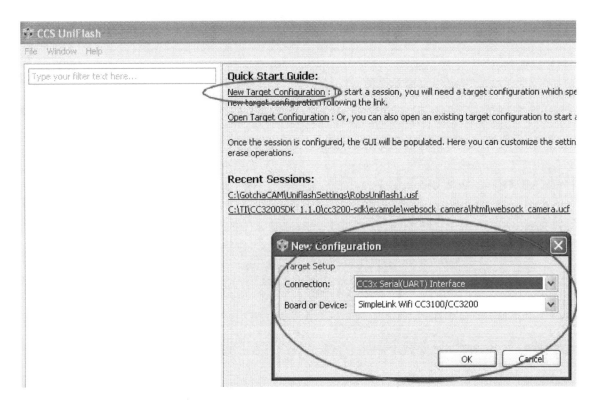

Figure 1-9. Setting up new target configuration

Formatting the Serial Flash

Generally the flash should come formatted. My ArduCAM CC3200 Uno board came with the flash formatted. However, if you need to reformat the serial flash, for example if the file system becomes corrupted and unusable then you can format the serial flash using Uniflash. Click the "Format" button from the main menu and select the capacity that you wish to format for. In the case of the ArduCAM CC3200 Uno you need to format the flash for 1MB of capacity. See Figure 1-10.

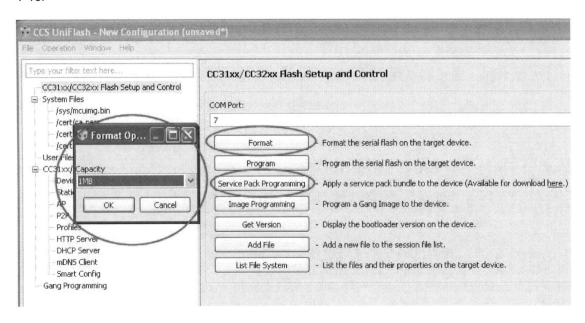

Figure 1-10. Formatting the Serial Flash

Also, if you format the serial flash you will need to install the service pack that is associated with the SDK using the "Service Pack Programming" button.

Setting up and Programming the MCU Image

The next thing to do is to select the file for the /sys/mcuimg.bin. Go to the left hand side and select the /sys/mcuimg.bin to bring up the screen that sets this file. Hit the "Browse" button, navigate to where the wlan_ap.bin file is, which should be in the Release directory under the project directory and select that as the Url. Also make sure you check "Erase", "Update" and "Verify". This will copy the file to the CC3200 when the Operation->Program menu selection is selected. See Figure 1-11.

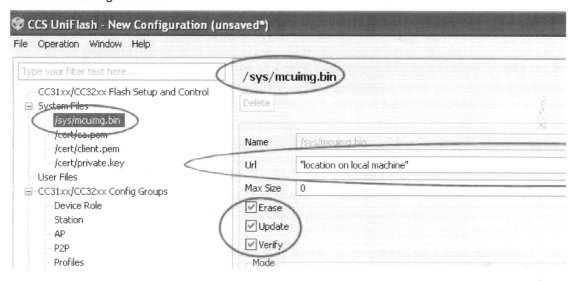

Figure 1-11. Setting the MCU Image

After the program has been copied to the device unplug the device from the USB port. Remove the jumper you placed on the SOP2 pins. Plug the device back into the USB port.

Starting and Setting up Terra Term

Next, start up Terra Term. When the program starts a popup appears. Select the "Serial" radio button and select the port that your CC3200 device is connected to from the dropdown box. See Figure 1-12.

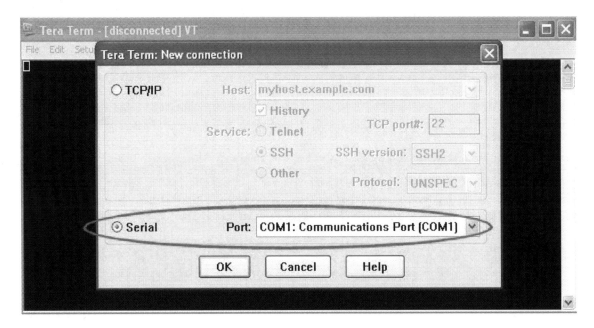

Figure 1-12. Selecting the Serial Port

Next, select the Setup->Serial Port menu to bring up a popup where you can set the COM port speed of the COM port that your CC3200 device is connected to. Select the 115200 speed. This is important. If you select a different speed you may not see the output from the CC3200 device. Then click the "OK" button. See Figure 1-13.

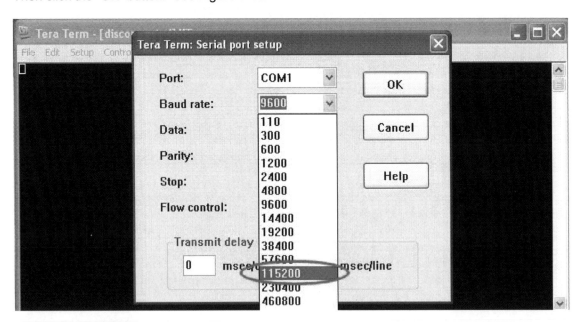

Figure 1-13. Selecting the Serial Port Speed

Running the Program

Next, press the reset button on the device. This will restart the program. See Figure 1-14.

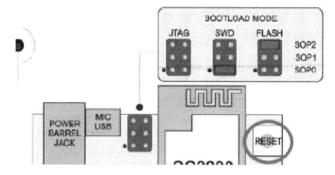

Figure 1-14. The reset button

After a few moments you should see text output from the program. When the line "Enter the AP SSID name" comes up enter a name for the access point and hit the enter key. The program will prompt you to connect a device to the CC3200. On your Android device go to the Settings-Wifi and turn on the Wifi if it is not already turned on. After the device has finished searching for new wifi access points the name of the CC3200 that you have just entered should appear.

Connect to the access point. The program running on the CC3200 will attempt to ping the Android device. The result of the ping will be output to the terminal and then the program will halt. See Figure 1-14.

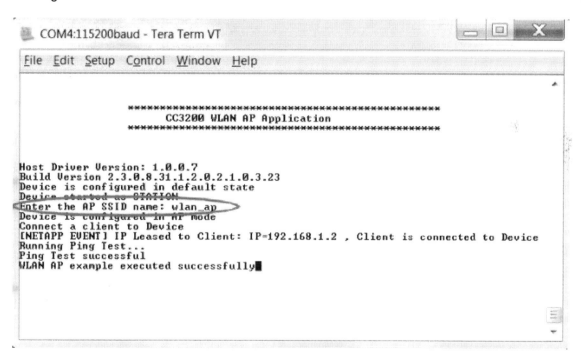

Figure 1-14. Input and Output to Terra Term

This example is very important because it is the basis for the program I present later in this book that accepts commands from the Android and sends picture data back to the Android device.

Summary

In this chapter I covered the basics of what you need to get started developing a wifi camera project using TI Code Composer Studio and the ArduCAM CC3200 Uno. I cover where to download and tips on installing the CC3200 SDK, TI Code Composer Studio, TI Real Time Operating System, Uniflash, TI Pinmux, and TerraTerm. Next, I list the key documentation you will need to develop programs using the CC3200 Simplelink chip. Finally, I present a "Hands on Example" where I guide the reader through compiling, burning to the CC3200 device, and running the wlan_ap example that demonstrates the CC3200 operating in access point mode.

Chapter 2

TI CC3200 SimpleLink Programming Language Basics

In this chapter I go over the basics of the CC3200 programming language which is actually the C/C++ programming language. I cover the basic elements of the C/C++ language that you will need in order to create programs that control the CC3200 board. Various key elements such as data types, constants, control loops, etc. are covered.

C Language Overview

The TI CC3200 uses C/C++ in its programs. This section briefly summaries key language elements. This is not meant as a reference guide and ideally you should have some experience with a programming language similar to C/C++.

Comments

- // - This is a single line comment that is used by the programmer to document the code. These comments are not executed.

- /* */ - These enclose a multi line comment that is used by the programmer to document the code. These comments are not executed.

Data Types

- void – This type being used with a function indicates that the function will not return any value to the function caller. For example, the main() function that is part of the standard code framework has a return type of void.

```
void main()

{

        // Put code here
```

```
}
```

- char – The char variable type can store character values and is 1 byte in length. The following code declares that tempchar is of type char and is an array with 50 elements.

  ```
  char tempchar[50];
  ```

- unsigned char – The unsigned char data type holds 1 byte of information in the range of 0 through 255.

- int – The int data type holds a 2 byte number in the range of -32,768 to 32,767.

- unsigned int – This data type is 2 bytes in length and holds a value from 0 to 65,535.

- long – This data type is 4 bytes in length and holds a value from -2,147,483,648 to 2,147,483,647.

- unsigned long – This data type is 4 bytes in length and holds a value between 0 to 4,294,967,295.

- float – This is a floating point number that is 4 bytes in length and holds a value between -3.4028235E+38 to 3.4028235E+38.

- array – An array is a continuous collection of data that can be accessed by an index number. Arrays are 0 based so that the first element in the array has an index of 0. Common types of arrays are character arrays, and integer arrays. The following code declares the variable Entries as an array of type char that contains 10 elements. The function ProcessRawCommandElement() is then called with element number 2 in the Entries array which is the third element in the array. Remember 0 is the first element in the array.

  ```
  char Entries[10];

  int success = ProcessRawCommandElement(Entries[2]);
  ```

The Define Statement

The define statement assigns a name to a constant value. During the compilation process the compiler will replace the constant name with the constant value. The following defines the CC3200 application's name as "Robs WLAN AP"

```
#define   APP_NAME        "Robs WLAN AP"
```

The Include Statement

The #include statement brings in code from outside files and "includes" them into your program. Generally a header or .h file is included which allows access to the functions and classes inside that file.

```
#include "simplelink.h"
```

The Semicolon

Each statement in C/C++ needs to end in a semicolon. For example, when declaring and initializing a variable you will need a semicolon.

```
const int chipSelect = 48;
```

Curly Braces

The curly braces such as { and } specify blocks of code and must match in pairs. That is, for every opening brace { there must be a closing brace } to match.

A function requires curly braces to denote the beginning and end of the function.

```
void Function1()

{

  // Body of Function

}
```

Program loops such as the for statement may also need the curly braces

```
for (int I = 0; I < 9; I++)

{

  // Body of loop

}
```

It is also good practice to use braces in control structures such as the if statement.

```
if (I < 0)

{

  // Body of If statement

}
```

Arithmetic Operators

- = - The equals sign is the assignment operator used to set a variable to a value. For example, the following sets the value of the variable Data to the result from the function CreatePhotoInfo().

  ```
  char* Data = CreatePhotoInfo();
  ```

- + - The plus sign performs addition.

  int NumberFilenames = NumberFileOpenJpeg + NumberFilesOpenRaw;

- - - The minus sign performs subtraction. For example, the following calculates the time it takes to capture a photo using the camera by measuring the difference between the starting time before the image is captured and the ending time just after the image is captured.

  ElapsedTime = TimeForCaptureEnd - TimeForCaptureStart;

- * - The asterisk sign performs multiplication. For example, the total bytes of an image is calculated by multiplying the width of the image by the height of the image by the bytes per pixel in the image.

  int TotalBytes = ImageWidth * ImageHeight * BytesPerPixel;

- / - The back slash sign performs division. For example, the speed in miles per hour of an object is calculated by dividing the number of miles the object has traveled by the number of hours that it took to travel that distance.

  float Speed = NumberMiles / NumberHours;

- % - The percent sign is the modulo operator that returns the remainder from a division between two integers. For example,

  int remainder = dividend % divisor;

Comparison Operators

- == - The double equal is a comparison operator to test if the argument on the left side of the double equal sign is equal to the argument on the right side. If the arguments are equal then it evaluates to true. Otherwise it evaluates to false. For example, if Command is equal to 1 then the code block is executed.

  if (Command == 1)

  {

         // Execute code

  }

- != - The exclamation point followed by an equal sign is the not equal to operator that evaluates to true if the argument on the left is not equal to the argument on the right side. Otherwise, it evaluates to false. For example, in the following code if the current camera resolution is not set to VGA then the code block is executed.

  if (Resolution != VGA)

  {

        // If current resolution is not VGA then set camera for VGA

}

- < - The less than operator evaluates to true if the argument on the left is less than the argument on the right. For example, in the code that follows the for loop will execute the code block while the height is less than the height of the photo. When the height counter becomes equal or greater than the photo's height then the loop exits.

```
for (int height = 0; height < PHOTO_HEIGHT; height++)

{

        // Process every row of the photo

}
```

- > - The greater than operator evaluates to true if the argument on the left side is greater than the argument on the right side.

```
if (Available() > 0)

{

        // Code Here

}
```

- <= - The less than sign followed by the equal sign returns true if the argument on the left hand side is less than or equal to the argument on the right hand side. It returns false otherwise.

- >= - The greater than sign followed by the equal sign returns true if the argument on the left is greater than or equal to the argument on the right. It returns false otherwise.

Boolean Operators

- && - This is the "and" boolean operator that only returns true if both the arguments on the left and right side evaluate to true. It returns false otherwise. For example, in the following code only if the previous value is 'O' and the current value is 'K' will the code block be executed. Otherwise it will not be executed.

```
char out,outprev = '$';

if ((outprev == 'O')&&(out == 'K'))

{

        out = ReadinData();

        // Code block

        outprev = out;
```

```
        }
```

- || - This is the "or" operator and returns true if either the left argument or the right argument evaluates to true. Otherwise, it returns false. For example, in the following code if either the camera's command is set to QQVGA or QVGA then the code block is executed. Otherwise it is not executed.

```
if ((Command == QQVGA) || (Command == QVGA))

{

        // Code

}
```

- ! – The not operator returns the opposite boolean value. The not value of true is false which is 0 and the not value of false is true which is non zero. In the following code a file is opened on the SD card and a pointer to the file is returned. If the pointer to the file is NULL which has a 0 value then not NULL would be 1 which is true. The if statement is executed when the argument is evaluated to true which means that the file pointer is NULL. This means that the open operation has failed and an error message needs to be displayed.

```
// Open File

InfoFile = SD.open(Filename.c_str(), FILE_WRITE);

// Test if file actually open

if (!InfoFile)

{

        Serial.println(F("\nCritical ERROR ... Can not open Photo Info File for output ... "));

        return;

}
```

Bitwise Operators

- & - This is the bitwise "and" operator between two numbers where each bit of each number has the "and" operation performed on it to produce the result in the final number. The resulting bit is 1 only if both bits in each number is 1. Otherwise the resulting bit is 0.

- | - This is the bitwise "or" operator between two numbers where each bit of each number has the "or" operation performed on it to produce the result in the final number. The resulting bit is 1 if the bit in either number is 1. Otherwise the resulting bit is 0.

- ^ - This is the bitwise "xor" operator between two numbers where each bit of each number has the "exclusive or" operation performed on it to produce the result in the final number. The resulting bit is 1 if the bits in each number are different and 0 otherwise.

- ~ - This is the bitwise "not" operator where each bit in the number following the "not" symbol is inverted. The resulting bit is 1 if the initial bit was 0 and the bit is 0 if the initial bit was 1.

- << - This is the bitshift left operator where each bit in the left operand is shifted to the left by the number of positions indicated by the right operand. For example, in the code below a 1 is shifted left PinPosition times and the final value is assigned to the variable ByteValue.

  ```
  ByteValue = 1 << PinPosition;
  ```

- >> - This is the bitshift right operator where each bit in the left operand is shifted to the right by the number of positions indicated by the right operand. For example, in the code below bits in the number 255 are shifted to the right PinPosition times and the final value is assigned to the variable ByteValue.

  ```
  ByteValue = 255 >> PinPosition;
  ```

Compound Operators

- ++ - This is the increment operator. The exact behavior of this operator also depends if it is placed before the variable being incremented or after the variable being incremented. In the following code the variable PhotoTakenCount is incremented by 1.

  ```
  PhotoTakenCount++;
  ```

  If the increment operator is placed after the variable being incremented then the variable is used first in the expression it is in before being incremented. For example, in the code below the height variable is used first in the for loop expression before it is incremented. So the first iteration of the for loop below would use height = 0. The height variable would be incremented after being used in the expression.

  ```
  for (int height = 0; height < PHOTO_HEIGHT; height++)

  {

          // Process row of image

  }
  ```

  If the increment operator is placed before variable being incremented then the variable is incremented first then it is used in the expression that it is in. For example, in the code below the height variable is incremented first before it is used in the for loop. This means that in the first iteration of the loop the height variable is 1 instead of 0.

  ```
  for (int height = 0; height < PHOTO_HEIGHT; ++height)

  {

          // Process row of image

  }
  ```

- -- - The decrement operator decrements a variable by 1 and its exact behavior depends on the placement of the operator either before or after the variable being decremented. If the operator is placed before the variable then the variable is decremented before being used in an expression. If the operator is placed after the variable then the variable is used in an expression before it is decremented. This follows the same pattern as the increment operator discussed previously.

- += - The compound addition operator adds the right operand to the left operand. This is actually a short hand version of

  operand1 = operand1 + operand2;

  Which is the same as the version that uses the compound addition operator.

  operand1 += operand2;

- -= - The compound subtraction operator subtracts the operand on the right from the operand on the left. For example, the code for a compound subtraction would be:

  operand1 -= operand2;

  This is the same as the following:

  operand1 = operand1 - operand2;

- *= - The compound multiplication operator multiplies the operand on the right by the operand on the left. The code for this is as follows.

  operand1 *= operand2;

  This is also equivalent to:

  operand1 = operand1 * operand2;

- /= - The compound division operator divides the operand on the left by the operand on the right. For example,

  operand1 /= operand2;

  This is equivalent to:

  operand1 = operand1 / operand2;

- &= - The compound bitwise and operator is equivalent to:

  x = x & y;

- != - The compound bitwise or operator is equivalent to:

  - x = x | y;

Pointer Access Operators

- * - The de-reference Operator allows you to access the contents that a pointer points to. For example, the code that follows declares a variable called pdata as a pointer to a byte and creates storage for the data using the new command. The pointer variable called pdata is then de-referenced to allow the actual data that the pointer points to be set to 1.

```
byte *pdata = new byte;

*pdata = 1;
```

- & - The address operator creates a pointer to a variable. For example, the following code declares a variable called data of type byte and assigns the value of 1 to it. A function called FunctionPointer() is defined that accepts as a parameter a pointer to a byte. In order to use this function with the variable data we need to call that function with a pointer to the variable data.

```
byte data = 1;

void FunctionPointer(byte *data)

{

   // body of function

}

FunctionPointer(&data);
```

Variable Scope

- Global variables – Global variables are variables that are declared outside any function and before they are used.

```
// VGA Default

int PHOTO_WIDTH = 640;

int PHOTO_HEIGHT = 480;

int PHOTO_BYTES_PER_PIXEL = 2;
```

- Local variables – Local variables are declared inside functions or code blocks and are only valid inside that function or code block. For example, in the following function the variable localnumber is only visible inside the Function1() function.

```
void Function1()

{

   int localnumber = 0;
```

```
}
```

Control Structures

- if (comparison operator) – The if statement is a control statement that tests if the result of the comparison operator or argument is true. If it is true then execute the code block. For example, in the following code the if statement tests to see if there is more data from the Bluetooth connection that needs to be read in. If there is then read the data in and assign it to the RawCommandLine variable.

```
if(BT.available() > 0)

{

        // If command is coming in then read it

        RawCommandLine = GetCommand();

        break;

}
```

- if (comparison operator) else – The if else control statement is similar to the if statement except with the addition of the else section which is executed if the previous if statement evaluates to false and is not executed. For example, in the following code if the frames per second parameter is set for 30 frames per second then the SetupCameraFor30FPS() function is called. Otherwise, if the frames per second parameter is set to night mode then the SetupCameraNightMode() function is called.

```
// Set FPS for Camera

if (FPSParam == ThirtyFPS)

{

    SetupCameraFor30FPS();

}

else

if (FPSParam == NightMode)

{

    SetupCameraNightMode();

}
```

- for (initialization; condition; increment) – The for statement is used to execute a code block usually initializing a counter then performing actions on a group of objects indexed by that incremented value. See the code example below.

```
for (int i = 0 ; i < NumberElements; i++)

{

    // Process Element i  Here

}
```

- while (expression) – The while statement executes a code block repeatedly until the expression evaluates to false. In the following code the while code block is executed as long as data is available for reading from the file.

```
// read from the file until there's nothing else in it:

while (TempFile.available())

{

    Serial.write(TempFile.read());

}
```

- break – A break statement is used to exit from a loop such as a while or for loop. In the following code the while loop causes the code block to be executed forever. If there is data available from the Serial Monitor then it is processed and then the while loop is exited.

```
while (1)

{

        if (Serial.available() > 0)

        {

                // Process the data

                break;

        }

}
```

- return (value) – The return statement exits a function. It also may return a value to the calling function.

```
return;

return false;
```

Summary

In this chapter I covered the basics of the CC3200 programming language. I covered a broad range of basic topics such as data types, constants, built in functions, and control loops. In addition, this chapter was not meant to be a reference manual but a quick start guide to the basics of the C programming language.

Chapter 3

The Android Controller and Wifi Communication

In this chapter I give an overview of Android development and Wifi communication. I discuss the various development software for Android such as the Android Studio and the Android ADT bundle and what hardware and software is required to develop applications for Android devices. Then I give a basic review of the Java programming language for Android. Finally, I discuss how I implemented wifi communication on Android. In terms of implementing wifi communication on the Android I cover the Client class and then the WifiMessageHandler class. The Client class initializes and connects the actual wifi to the CC3200. The WifiMessageHandler class processes incoming data from the CC3200.

What is an Android?

The Android is a mobile operating system for cell phones and tablets. Android equipped devices are generally low cost and widely available which makes them the ideal device to use in a wireless home security system. Additionally many Android phones can be operated based on a month to month basis with no long term contract to sign. This is also ideal for an on demand type security system where you can scale up or down based on the need. For example, if the area where you live has experienced a series of thefts you can set up the burglar alarm security system described in this book. You can then activate the cell phone service for your Android phone so that if an intruder breaks into your home you can have the Android set to call out to an emergency number that you can designate to alert you of the possible break in. You can hide your Android in a location near areas that burglars might be interested in such as a home theater system and listen in to see if you hear any unusual activity. In this case you would probably hear the thieves moving the electronic equipment around so this would confirm that there is an actual break in. You would then call the police and report the crime as a burglary in progress. You can also send out emergency text message alerts to your cell phone when the alarm is tripped.

Getting Started with Android Development

In this section we cover the different development environments available for Android development. First I cover the Android Studio development environment which is the newest. The Eclipse with ADT plug-ins is covered next along with the Eclipse ADT Bundle which is the preferred version of the Eclipse with ADT plug-ins.

Android Studio

Android Studio is the newest Android development system available and is recommended by Google.

System Requirements:

Windows

- Microsoft® Windows® 8/7/Vista (32 or 64-bit)

- 2 GB RAM minimum, 4 GB RAM recommended

- 400 MB hard disk space

- At least 1 GB for Android SDK, emulator system images, and caches

- 1280 x 800 minimum screen resolution

- Java Development Kit (JDK) 7

- Optional for accelerated emulator: Intel® processor with support for Intel® VT-x, Intel® EM64T (Intel® 64), and Execute Disable (XD) Bit functionality

Mac OS X

- Mac® OS X® 10.8.5 or higher, up to 10.9 (Mavericks)

- 2 GB RAM minimum, 4 GB RAM recommended

- 400 MB hard disk space

- At least 1 GB for Android SDK, emulator system images, and caches

- 1280 x 800 minimum screen resolution

- Java Runtime Environment (JRE) 6

- Java Development Kit (JDK) 7

- Optional for accelerated emulator: Intel® processor with support for Intel® VT-x, Intel® EM64T (Intel® 64), and Execute Disable (XD) Bit functionality

- On Mac OS, run Android Studio with Java Runtime Environment (JRE) 6 for optimized font rendering. You can then configure your project to use Java Development Kit (JDK) 6 or JDK 7.

Linux

- GNOME or KDE desktop

- GNU C Library (glibc) 2.15 or later

- 2 GB RAM minimum, 4 GB RAM recommended

- 400 MB hard disk space

- At least 1 GB for Android SDK, emulator system images, and caches

- 1280 x 800 minimum screen resolution

- Oracle® Java Development Kit (JDK) 7

- Tested on Ubuntu® 14.04, Trusty Tahr (64-bit distribution capable of running 32-bit applications).

Note: The official web page for Android Studio is
http://developer.android.com/tools/studio/index.html

Eclipse with Android Development Tools (ADT)

All the Android project examples for this book were created in the Eclipse development environment using the Android Development Tools (ADT) plug-ins. This has an advantage that it works with older operating systems such as Windows XP. In fact inexpensive Windows XP systems can be bought on sites such as Ebay and Amazon.com. If you are starting from scratch and want an affordable system to develop Android applications then you should consider getting a Windows XP based computer system for Android as well as CC3200 development.

Android development using the Eclipse with Android Development Tools plug-ins can be done on a Windows PC, Mac OS machine, or a Linux machine. The exact operating system requirements are as follows:

Operating Systems:

- Windows XP (32-bit), Vista (32- or 64-bit), or Windows 7 (32- or 64-bit)

- Mac OS X 10.5.8 or later (x86 only)

- Linux (tested on Ubuntu Linux, Lucid Lynx)

- GNU C Library (glibc) 2.7 or later is required.

- On Ubuntu Linux, version 8.04 or later is required.

- 64-bit distributions must be capable of running 32-bit applications.

Developing Android programs also requires installation of the Java Development Kit. Java Development Kit requirements are JDK 6 or later and are located at www.oracle.com/technetwork/java/javase/downloads/index.html.

If you are using a Mac, then Java may already be installed.

The Eclipse IDE program modified with the Android Development Tools (ADT) plug-in forms the basis for the Android development environment. The requirements for Eclipse are as follows:

- Eclipse 3.6.2 (Helios) or greater located at http://eclipse.org

- Eclipse JDT plug-in (included in most Eclipse IDE packages)

- Android Development Tools (ADT) plug-in for Eclipse located at http://developer.android.com/tools/sdk/eclipse-adt.html

---

Note: Eclipse 3.5 (Galileo) is no longer supported with the latest version of ADT. For the latest information on Android development tools, go to http://developer.android.com/tools/index.html.

The official web page for Android Eclipse Android Development Tools (ADT) plug ins was on http://developer.android.com/tools/help/adt.html

---

Eclipse ADT Bundle Download

If you are going to use the Eclipse with ADT plug-ins for your development then I suggest downloading the ADT Bundle which is basically a zip file that consists of a version of Eclipse with the ADT plug-ins already installed. All you would need to do is uncompress the zip file and create a shortcut to the "eclipse.exe" file that is in one of the directories inside the bundle.

The ADT Bundle is available for the Windows, Mac, and Linux operating systems at the following links that were working as this sentence is being typed. You can also search for "android adt bundle" using a search engine like Google or Yahoo to get the latest results.

Win 32 Bit:

https://dl.google.com/android/adt/adt-bundle-windows-x86-20140702.zip

Win 64 Bit:

https://dl.google.com/android/adt/adt-bundle-windows-x86_64-20140702.zip

Mac 64 Bit:

http://dl.google.com/android/adt/adt-bundle-mac-x86_64-20140702.zip

Linux 32 Bit:

http://dl.google.com/android/adt/adt-bundle-linux-x86-20140702.zip

Linux 64 Bit:

http://dl.google.com/android/adt/adt-bundle-linux-x86_64-20140702.zip

Migrating To Android Studio from Eclipse ADT

The Android Studio is the new "official" development environment for Android programs and replaces the Eclipse ADT system which will no longer be supported in terms of support for new versions of the Android operating system. However, for our purposes the older Eclipse ADT is fine and all the Android projects in this book were creating using the older Eclipse ADT bundle.

To migrate existing Android projects, simply import them using Android Studio:

1. In Android Studio, close any projects currently open. You should see the Welcome to Android Studio window.

2. Click Import Non-Android Studio project.

3. Locate the project you exported from Eclipse, expand it, select the build.gradle file and click OK.

4. In the following dialog, leave the "Use gradle wrapper" selected and click "OK". (You do not need to specify the Gradle home.)

5. Android Studio properly updates the project structure and creates the appropriate Gradle build file.

For a more full summary and additional information about migrating your Eclipse ADT project to the newest version of Android Studio visit the official web page for migration as shown below in the following important note.

> Note: The official web page for migrating code from the Android Eclipse ADT to the new Android Studio was on http://developer.android.com/sdk/installing/migrate.html

Overview of the Java Language

This section on the Java language is intended as a quick start guide to someone who has some knowledge of computer programming as well as some knowledge about object oriented programming. This section is NOT intended to be a Java reference manual. It is also not intended to cover every feature of the Java programming language.

The Java language for Android is run on a Java virtual machine. This means that the same compiled Java Android program can run on many different Android phones with different central processing unit (CPU) types. This is a key feature in terms of future expandability to faster processing units including those that will be specifically designed to enhance 3d games. The trade off to this is speed. Java programs run slower than programs compiled for a CPU in its native machine language since a Java virtual machine must interpret the code and then execute it on the native processor. A program that is already compiled for a specific native processor does not need to be interpreted and can save execution time by skipping this step.

Java Comments

- Single Line Comments – Single line comments start with two "//" slash characters.

  // This is a Single Line Java Comment

- Multi Line Comments – Multi line comments start with a "/*" slash followed by an asterisk and end in a "*/" an asterisk followed by a slash.

```
/*
      This is
      a Multi-Line
      Comment
*/
```

Java Basic Data Types

- byte – A 8 bit number with values from –128 to 127 inclusive.

- short – A 16 bit number with values from -32,768 to 32,767 inclusive.

- int - A 32 bit number with values from -2,147,483,648 to 2,147,483,647 inclusive.

- long – A 64 bit number with values from -9,223,372,036,854,775,808 to 9,223,372,036,854,775,807 inclusive.

- float - A single-precision 32-bit IEEE 754 floating point number.

- double – A double-precision 64-bit IEEE 754 floating point number.

- char - A single 16-bit Unicode character that has a range of '\u0000' (or 0) to '\uffff' (or 65,535 inclusive).

- boolean – Has a value of either true or false.

Arrays

In Java you can create arrays of elements from the basic Java data types listed above. The following statement creates an array of m_DataSize elements of type byte.

```
int       m_DataSize  = 700000;

byte[]    m_DataByte = new byte[m_DataSize];
```

Data Modifiers

- private – Variables that are private are only accessible from within the class they are declared in.

- public – Variables that are public can be accessed from any class.

- static – Variables that are declared static have only one copy associated with the class they are declared in.

- final – The final modifier indicates that the variable will not change.

Java Operators

Arithmetic Operators

- \+   Additive operator (also used for String concatenation)

- \-   Subtraction operator

- *   Multiplication operator

- /   Division operator

- %   Remainder operator

Unary Operators

- \+   Unary plus operator

- \-   Negates an expression

- ++   Increments a value by 1

- --   Decrements a value by 1

- !   Inverts the value of a boolean

Conditional Operators

- &&   Conditional-AND

- || Conditional-OR

- =   Assignment operator

- ==   Equal to

- !=   Not equal to

- \>   Greater than

- \>=   Greater than or equal to

- \<   Less than

- \<=   Less than or equal to

Bitwise and Bit Shift Operators

- ~   Unary bitwise complement

- <<   Signed left shift

- \>>   Signed right shift

- \>>>   Unsigned right shift

- &   Bitwise AND

- ^   Bitwise exclusive OR

- | Bitwise inclusive OR

Java Flow Control Statements

- if then statement

```
if (expression)
{

        // execute statements here if expression evaluates to true

}
```

- if then else statement

```
if (expression)

{

        // execute statements here if expression evaluates to true

}

else

{
```

```
            // execute statements here if expression evaluates to false

    }
```

- **switch statement**

```
switch(expression)

{

        case label1:

                // Statements to execute if expression evaluates to

                // label1:

        break;


        case label2:

                // Statements to execute if expression evaluates to

                // label2:

        break;

}
```

- **while statement**

```
while (expression)

{

        // Statements here execute as long as expression evaluates // to true;

}
```

- **for statement**

```
for (variable counter initialization;  expression;  variable counter increment/decrement)

{

        // variable counter initialized when for loop is first

        // executed


        // Statements here execute as long as expression is true
```

```
        // counter variable is updated

    }
```

Java Classes

Java is an object oriented language. What this means is that you can derive or extend existing classes to form new customized classes of the existing classes. The derived class will have all the functionality of the parent class in addition to any new functions that you may want to add in.

The following class is a customized version of its parent class from which it derives which is the Activity class. The MainActivity class will be the main and most important class we will be dealing with on the Android side of this book. All of our other custom classes are executed directly or indirectly from the MainActivity class.

```
public class MainActivity extends Activity

{

        // Body of class

}
```

Packages and Classes

Packages are a way in Java to group together classes, and interfaces that are related in some way. For example, a package can represent a single application.

```
package com.example.bluetoothtest;
```

Accessing Classes in Packages

In order to access classes that are located in other packages you have to bring them into view using the "import" statement. For example, in order to use the Log class that is located inside the android.util.Log package you need to import it with the following statement.

```
import android.util.Log;
```

Then, you can use the class definition without the full package name such as:

```
Log.e("error", "This Language is not supported");
```

To print out an error message to the Log debug window in the Eclipse development environment.

Accessing Class Variables and Functions

You can access a class's variables and functions through the "." operator just like in C++. See some examples below.

BluetoothMessageHandler   m_BluetoothMessageHandler = null;

m_PhotoData = m_BluetoothMessageHandler.GetBinaryData();

m_BluetoothMessageHandler.ResetData();

m_BluetoothMessageHandler.SetCommand(Command);

String Data = m_BluetoothMessageHandler.GetStringData();

Java Functions

The general format for Java functions is the same as in other languages such as C/C++. The function heading starts with optional modifiers such as private, public, or static. Next is a return value that can be void if there is no return value or a basic data type or and class. This is followed by the function name and then the parameter list.

Modifiers Return_value FunctionName(ParameterType1 Parameter1, ...)

```
{

        // Code Body

}
```

Calling the Parent Function

A function in a derived class can override the function in the parent or superclass using the @Override annotation. This is not required but helps to prevent programming errors. If the intention is to override a parent function but the function does not in fact do this then a compiler error will be generated.

In order for the function in a derived class to actually call its corresponding function in the parent class you use the super prefix as seen below.

```
@Override

public void onCreate(Bundle savedInstanceState)

{

        super.onCreate(savedInstanceState);

        // Put new original code here

}
```

Note: Additional Java tutorials can be found on http://docs.oracle.com/javase/tutorial/

Java Interfaces

The purpose of a Java interface is to provide a standard way for programmers to implement the actual functions in an interface in code in a derived class. An interface does not contain any actual code just the function definitions. The function bodies with the actual code must be defined by other classes that implement that interface. For example, the MainActivity class in the examples in this book implements the Runnable interface in order for code in other classes to change the Android's User Interface. In order to do this the run() function must be defined in the MainActivity class.

```java
public class MainActivity extends Activity implements Runnable

{

        public void run()

        {

                // Original code to implement the Runnable interface

        }

}
```

Overview of Wifi for Android

This section covers key issues involving establishing a wifi connection with another device. I first discuss the permissions you will need to give the Android device. I then discuss the general client/server design of the home security system presented in this book. Next, I cover how wifi is initialized from the MainActivity class. I then discuss how a wifi connection is implemented using the Client class. Finally, I cover the WifiMessageHandler class that is used to process incoming data from the CC3200 device.

Wifi Permissions

In order to use the Android Wifi to connect to the CC3200 device we need to add some permissions in the AndroidManifest.xml file.

These permissions allow you to turn the Android's wifi on and off.

```xml
<uses-permission android:name="android.permission.ACCESS_WIFI_STATE"/>
```

```xml
<uses-permission android:name="android.permission.CHANGE_WIFI_STATE"/>
```

Permissions are also required to access and change the Android's connection state to a network such as when connecting to the CC3200 in Access Point mode.

```xml
<uses-permission android:name="android.permission.ACCESS_NETWORK_STATE"/>
```

```xml
<uses-permission android:name="android.permission.CHANGE_NETWORK_STATE"/>
```

Also, in order to send and receive data on the newly created network between the CC3200 and the Android device you will need to give the Android permission to access the internet.

```
<uses-permission android:name="android.permission.INTERNET"/>
```

In order to keep the Android's wifi radio turned on all the time we need to add the wake lock permission.

```
<uses-permission android:name="android.permission.WAKE_LOCK"/>
```

Basic Android/CC3200 Client/Server Design

The general setup for the home security system presented in this book is to have the TI CC3200 serve as the server or slave device that runs a TCP server and listens for an incoming connection from a client device which is the Android. The Android sends commands to the CC3200 and the CC3200 responds to these commands by sending data back to the Android. See Figure 3-1.

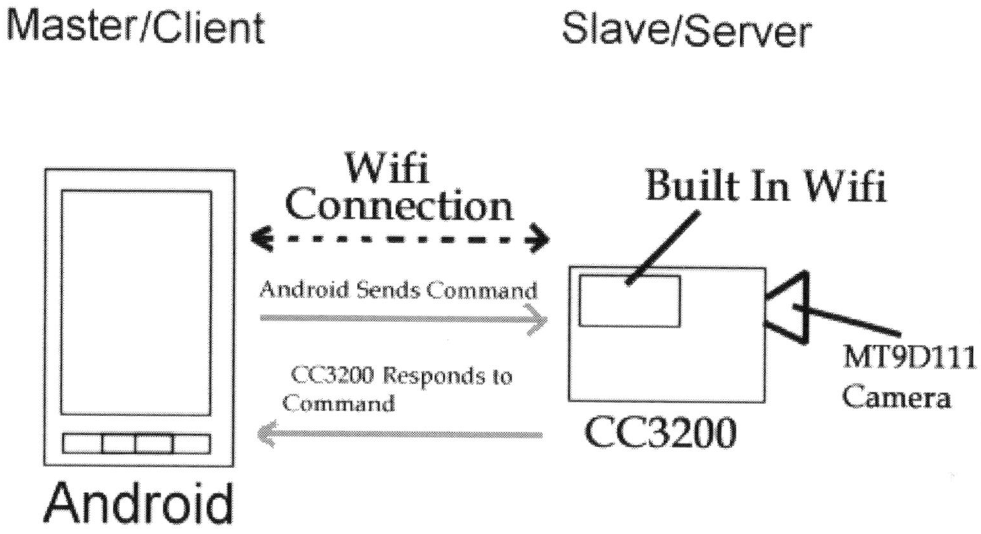

Figure 3-1. The basic home security system design

Initializing Wifi for Android

Wifi is initialized and setup in the MainActivity class on the Android side.

For our Android program we will connect the Android to a TCP server that is running on the CC3200 side.

The IP address of the CC3200 is static and is set to 10.1.1.1 and is held in the following variable.

```
String m_ServerStaticIP = "10.1.1.1";
```

The port number of the server that is running on the CC3200 device is 5001 and is held on the Android side in the variable m_PortNumber.

```
int m_PortNumber= 5001;
```

The Android's client thread will be held in the m_ClientConnectThread variable.

m_ClientConnectThread=null;

The CreateClientConnection() function creates the Android client that will connect to the CC3200 Tcp server by:

1. Creating a new WifiMessageHandler class object with the input parameter of this instance of the MainActivity class.

2. Creating a new Client class object and initializing it with the Ip address of the server, the port number that the server is listening to, the wifi message handler object m_WifiMessageHandler, and the current instance of the MainActivity object.

3. If the m_ClientConnectThread is not null then display a message on the Android's debug window that the client thread is starting.

4. Start executing the client thread by calling the m_ClientConnectThread.start() function.

See Listing 3-1.

Listing 3-1. The CreateClientConnection() function

```
void CreateClientConnection(String ServerStaticIP, int PortNumber)

{

        m_WifiMessageHandler = new WifiMessageHandler(this);

        m_ClientConnectThread = new Client(ServerStaticIP, PortNumber, m_WifiMessageHandler, this);

        if (m_ClientConnectThread != null)

        {

                AddDebugMessage(TAG + ": Starting ClientConnectThread ...\n");

                m_ClientConnectThread.start();

        }

}
```

In the MainActivity class's onCreate() function, the function to create the client thread which is CreateClientConnection() is called with the ip address and port number of the server running on the CC32000 device.

CreateClientConnection(m_ServerStaticIP, m_PortNumber);

Connecting to a TI CC3200 Simplelink Device with Wifi using the Client Class

The Client class is a custom class I created that extends the Thread class which is a standard built in Android class.

```
public class Client extends Thread
```

The important thing to take notice of here is that this class is a thread which executes separately from the MainActivity thread that controls the GUI (Graphical User Interface). Also, in some versions of Android all wifi activity must be in a thread other than the MainActivity thread. The reason being that wifi activity can block other functions such as processing user input so that the user would incorrectly believe that the application has stopped working.

The TAG variable is a String that is used in combination with the Log() function to indicate that it is the Client class that Log() debug output print statements belong to.

```
String TAG = "CLIENT";
```

The key class to manage and control the Android's wifi is called the WifiManager class represented by the variable m_WifiManager.

```
WifiManager m_WifiManager = null;
```

In order to keep the Android's wifi on continuously even when the screen goes dark we need to use the WifiLock class represented by the m_WifiLock variable.

```
WifiLock m_WifiLock = null;
```

In order to retrieve information about the Android's current wifi connection we need to use the WifiInfo class which is represented by the variable m_WifiInfo.

```
WifiInfo m_WifiInfo = null;
```

The MacAddress of the Android device is held in the variable m_MacAddress.

```
String m_MacAddress = "";
```

The speed of the current wifi connection is held in the variable m_LinkSpeed.

```
int m_LinkSpeed = 0;
```

In order to determine if the Android's wifi is actually connected to the CC3200 we need to use the ConnectivityManager class.

```
ConnectivityManager m_ConnectivityManager = null;
```

The m_WifiConnectInfo variable holds information relating to the state of the Android's wifi connection with the CC3200.

```
NetworkInfo m_WifiConnectInfo = null;
```

The access point's SSID which is the name for the access point located on the CC3200 is held in the m_SSID variable as a String object.

```
String m_SSID = "";
```

The ip address of the server to connect to is held in the m_ServerIPAddressString variable.

```
String     m_ServerIPAddressString = "";
```

The port number for the server that is running on the CC3200 device is held in the m_ServerPortNumber variable.

int m_ServerPortNumber = 0;

The IP address of the Android phone that serves as the client received from the WifiManager class is stored here.

int m_ClientIPAddress = -1;

The m_ClientIPAddressString holds the IP address that was stored in m_ClientIPAddress in String format instead of integer format.

String m_ClientIPAddressString = "";

The m_ClientIPByteArray variable holds the Android's IP address in byte array format.

byte[] m_ClientIPByteArray = null;

The m_Socket variable holds the Android Socket object that will be used to connect to the CC3200's TCP server.

Socket m_Socket = null;

The m_IsConnected variable is true is the Android client is connected to the server on the CC3200 and false otherwise.

volatile boolean m_IsConnected = false;

The m_SocketOutputStream variable is an OutputStream class object that is used to send data from the Android to the CC3200 device.

OutputStream m_SocketOutputStream = null;

The m_SocketInputStream variable is an InputStream class object that is used to read in data from the CC3200 device.

InputStream m_SocketInputStream = null;

The m_WifiMessageHandler variable handles the incoming data from the CC3200 based upon the command that was initially sent to the CC3200 device from the Android device.

WifiMessageHandler m_WifiMessageHandler = null;

The m_MainActivity variable holds a reference to the MainActivity class object that created this Client object instance.

MainActivity m_MainActivity = null;

The m_Freeze variable stops the execution of the thread if it is true. This variable is declared volatile so that a different thread can set this variable and this thread will see this variable change to the new value.

volatile boolean m_Freeze = false;

The run() Function

The run() function is executed when the start() function is called on the thread.

The run() function sets up the wifi, creates the client socket on the Android side, handles the connection to the CC3200, and continually reads in and processes incoming wifi data from the CC3200 device. The run() function does this by:

1. Calling the InitWifiManager() function to initialize the wifi manager class object on the Android device.

2. Continuously checking to see if the Android has been connected to a wifi network. If it has not then check to see if the thread should be stopped. If the thread should be stopped then return from the run() function and stop execution. Otherwise, suspend program execution for 1000 milliseconds and then repeat step 2.

3. Retrieve the connection information for the currently connected wifi connection by calling the GetWifiConnectionInfo() function.

4. If the information was successfully retrieved from step 3 then call the DisplayWifiConnectionInfoDebug() function to display the wifi connection information on the Android program's debug window. Otherwise, exit out the run() function and print out an error using the Log() function.

5. Create a client socket and try to connect this to the server ip address and server port on the CC3200 by calling the CreateConnectSocket() function.

6. If the Android and CC3200 are connected by wifi then start to read in incoming data. Otherwise exit out the run() function.

7. In order to read in data from the CC3200 the program:

    1. Creates an array of bytes called "buffer" of length 1024.

    2. Creates an integer variable called "bytes" that holds the number of bytes that are read from the wifi connection.

    3. Reads in the incoming data from the wifi connection to the CC3200 device by calling the m_SocketInputStream.read(buffer) function with the buffer created in step 1. The function returns the number of bytes read and stores this in the bytes variable.

    4. Calls the m_WifiMessageHandler.ReceiveMessage(bytes, buffer) function which processes the incoming data using the m_WifiMessageHandler variable. The two input parameters are the number of bytes read in from step 3 and the buffer created in step 1.

    5. If there is an error reading in the data using the read() command in step 3 then an exception is thrown and the run() function is exited.

See Listing 3-2.

Listing 3-2. The run() function

@Override

```
public void run()

{

        // Init Wifi

        InitWifiManager();


        // Check for Network Connectivity

        while (!IsConnectedToWifi())

        {

                // If thread has been frozen then stop execution and return from run() function

                if (m_Freeze)

                {

                        return;

                }


                // while wifi is not connected then do nothing.

                try {

                        sleep(1000);

                } catch (InterruptedException e) {

                        // TODO Auto-generated catch block

                        Log.e(TAG, "Sleep Command FAILED !!!!");

                        e.printStackTrace();

                }

        }


        if (GetWifiConnectionInfo())

        {

                DisplayWifiConnectionInfoDebug();

        }

        else
```

```
    {
            // Get Wifi Connection Info Failed.

            Log.e(TAG, "Getting Wifi Connection Info Failed !!!");

            return;

    }


    // Try to Connect Socket to Server

    CreateConnectSocket();


    // If connection is not successfull then return

    if (!m_IsConnected)

    {
            return;

    }


    // Continuously read in data from CC3200

    byte[] buffer = new byte[1024];  // buffer store for the stream

    int bytes; // number bytes returned from read()


    // Keep listening to the InputStream until an exception occurs

    while (m_IsConnected)

    {
            try

            {
                    // Read from the InputStream

                    bytes = m_SocketInputStream.read(buffer);


                    // Send the obtained bytes to the UI activity

                    m_WifiMessageHandler.ReceiveMessage(bytes, buffer);
```

```
            }

        catch (IOException e)

            {

                    Log.e(TAG, "Error Reading Wifi DATA ... ERROR = " + e.toString());

                    break;

            }

        }

    }
```

The InitWifiManager() Function

The InitWifiManger() function initializes the Android's wifi by:

1. Creating a new WifiManager object by calling the
    m_MainActivity.getSystemService(MainActivity.WIFI_SERVICE) function and setting the
    result to the m_WifiManager variable.

2. Creating a new ConnectivityManager object by calling the
    m_MainActivity.getSystemService(MainActivity.CONNECTIVITY_SERVICE) function and
    setting the result to the m_ConnectivityManager variable.

3. If the Android's wifi is enabled then set a debug message to be printed out on the Android's
    debug message window indicating that the wifi is on.

4. If the Android's wifi is not enabled then turn on the Android's wifi by calling the
    m_WifiManager.setWifiEnabled(true) function with the parameter true and then set a debug
    message to be displayed in the debug message window indicating that the wifi is being
    turned on.

5. If this thread instance has not been stopped by setting m_Freeze to true then update the
    program's user interface by calling the m_MainActivity.runOnUiThread(m_MainActivity)
    function. This calls the MainActivity class's run() function which will update the user interface
    data with the changes from the Client class.

See Listing 3-3.

Listing 3-3. The InitWifiManager() Function

```
void InitWifiManager()

{

        m_WifiManager = (WifiManager) m_MainActivity.getSystemService(MainActivity.WIFI_SERVICE);

        m_ConnectivityManager =
(ConnectivityManager)m_MainActivity.getSystemService(MainActivity.CONNECTIVITY_SERVICE);
```

```
if (m_WifiManager.isWifiEnabled())

{

        m_MainActivity.AddDebugMessageThread("Wifi is on ..." + "\n");

}

else

{

        m_WifiManager.setWifiEnabled(true);

        m_MainActivity.AddDebugMessageThread("Wifi is NOT on. Turning on Wifi ..." + "\n");

}


if (m_Freeze == false)

{

        // Update the User Interface

        m_MainActivity.runOnUiThread(m_MainActivity);

}

}
```

The IsConnectedToWifi() Function

The IsConnectedToWifi() function returns true if the Android is connected to the CC3200 server through wifi and returns false otherwise.

This function does the following:

1. First gets the current wifi network information through the connectivity manager by using the getNetworkInfo(ConnectivityManager.TYPE_WIFI) function which retrieves the current wifi connection information.

2. Returns the wifi connection state by calling the m_WifiConnectInfo.isConnected() function and returning the result.

See Listing 3-4.

Listing 3-4. The IsConnectedToWifi() function

```
boolean IsConnectedToWifi()
```

```
{

        m_WifiConnectInfo = m_ConnectivityManager.getNetworkInfo(ConnectivityManager.TYPE_WIFI);

        return m_WifiConnectInfo.isConnected();

}
```

The GetWifiConnectionInfo() Function

The GetWifiConnectionInfo() function gets information regarding the Android's wifi connection to the CC3200 device.

This function does the following:

1. If the Android's wifi is enabled then:

    1. The connection information structure containing all the network connection information is retrieved by calling the m_WifiManager.getConnectionInfo() function and is stored in the m_WifiInfo variable.

    2. The speed of the wifi connection is retrieved by calling the m_WifiInfo.getLinkSpeed() function.

    3. The IP address of the Android is retrieved by calling the m_WifiInfo.getIpAddress() function.

    4. The access point's name is retrieved by calling the m_WifiInfo.getSSID() function.

    5. The Android device's MAC address is retrieved by calling the m_WifiInfo.getMacAddress() function.

    6. If the wifi connection information has been retrieved then true is returned otherwise false is returned.

See Listing 3-5.

Listing 3-5. The GetWifiConnectionInfo() Function

```
boolean GetWifiConnectionInfo()

{

        boolean result = false;

        if (m_WifiManager.isWifiEnabled())

        {

                //WifiInfo           getConnectionInfo()

                //Return dynamic information about the current Wi-Fi connection, if any is active.
```

```
        m_WifiInfo = m_WifiManager.getConnectionInfo();


        // Get Wifi Connection Info

        m_LinkSpeed          =         m_WifiInfo.getLinkSpeed();

        m_ClientIPAddress    =         m_WifiInfo.getIpAddress();

        m_SSID               =         m_WifiInfo.getSSID();

        m_MacAddress         =         m_WifiInfo.getMacAddress();


        result = true;

    }

    return result;

}
```

The DisplayWifiConnectionInfoDebug() Function

The DisplayWifiConnectionInfoDebug() function displays the current wifi connection information inside the debug window of the Android application.

The DisplayWifiConnectionInfoDebug() function does the following:

1. Converts the Android's client IP address from a number to a String object by calling the ConvertClientIPAddressToString(m_ClientIPAddress) function with the numerical version of the IP address retrieved previously in the GetWifiConnectionInfo() function.

2. Sets up for the printing of the client IP address to the debug window.

3. Sets up for the printing of the static IP address of the CC3200 to the debug window.

4. Gets the IP address associated with the CC3200 server by calling the InetAddress.getAllByName(m_ServerIPAddressString) function with the String value of the server's IP address and setting the IA variable to the first element of the returned array. The IA variable now holds the internet address of the server in the form of an InetAddress class object.

5. If the IA variable is not null then set up for the printing of the server ip address.

6. Sets up for the printing of the access point's SSID to the debug window.

7. Sets up for the printing of the link speed and the Android's mac address to the debug window.

8. If the thread has not been halted by setting the m_Freeze variable to true then do the actual update of the debug window by calling the m_MainActivity.runOnUiThread(m_MainActivity) function which executes the run() function in the MainActivity class.

58

See Listing 3-6.

Listing 3-6. The DisplayWifiConnectionInfoDebug() Function

```
void DisplayWifiConnectionInfoDebug()

{

        m_ClientIPAddressString = ConvertClientIPAddressToString(m_ClientIPAddress);

        m_MainActivity.AddDebugMessageThread("Android Client IP Address: " + m_ClientIPAddressString +
"\n");


        // AP Info

        m_MainActivity.AddDebugMessageThread("AP/CC3200 Static IP Address: " + m_ServerIPAddressString +
"\n");


        InetAddress IA = null;

        try {

                IA = InetAddress.getAllByName(m_ServerIPAddressString)[0];

        } catch (UnknownHostException e) {

                m_MainActivity.AddDebugMessageThread(TAG + ": Can not get Server InetAddress from
getAllByName(), Error = " + e.toString()  +  "\n");

                e.printStackTrace();

        }

        if (IA != null)

        {

                m_MainActivity.AddDebugMessageThread("Access Point Name: " + IA.getHostName() + "\n");

        }

        m_MainActivity.AddDebugMessageThread("Access Point SSID: " + m_SSID + "\n");


        // Connection Info

        m_MainActivity.AddDebugMessageThread("Link Speed: " + m_LinkSpeed + "\n");

        m_MainActivity.AddDebugMessageThread("Android Client MacAddress: " + m_MacAddress + "\n");
```

```
            if (m_Freeze == false)

            {

                    // Update the User Interface

                    m_MainActivity.runOnUiThread(m_MainActivity);

            }

    }
```

The ConvertClientIPAddressToString() Function

The ConvertClientIPAddressToString() function converts an ip address that is in integer format into one that is in String format and then returns it.

The ConvertClientIPAddressToString() function does the following:

1. If the input ip address is in little endian format then reverse the bytes in the number to big endian format. Big endian format is where the most significant byte in the number is stored in the lowest memory location and the least significant byte is stored in the highest memory location.

2. Convert the ip address into an array of bytes and store it in the m_ClientIPByteArray variable by calling the BigInteger.valueOf(IPAddress).toByteArray() function with the ip address as the parameter.

3. Get the InetAddress class object representation of the ip address by calling the InetAddress.getByAddress(m_ClientIPByteArray) function with the byte array calculated in step 2. Then get the String representation by calling the getHostAddress() function of the InetAddress class object.

4. If there is an exception then write out error messages by calling the Log() function and the m_MainActivity.AddDebugMessageThread() to add an error message to the debug window.

5. Return the String representation of the ip address that was input to the function.

See Listing 3-7.

Listing 3-7. The ConvertClientIPAddressToString() function

```
String ConvertClientIPAddressToString(int IPAddress)

{

        String result = "N/A";


        // Convert little-endian to big-endian if needed
```

```
if (ByteOrder.nativeOrder().equals(ByteOrder.LITTLE_ENDIAN))

{

        IPAddress = Integer.reverseBytes(IPAddress);

}


m_ClientIPByteArray = BigInteger.valueOf(IPAddress).toByteArray();

try {

    result = InetAddress.getByAddress(m_ClientIPByteArray).getHostAddress();

} catch (UnknownHostException ex) {

    Log.e("CLIENT", "Unable to get host address from Network Byte Array...");

    m_MainActivity.AddDebugMessageThread(TAG + ":Unable to get host address from Network Byte
Array...\n");

    return result;

}


return result;

}
```

The CreateConnectSocket() Function

The CreateConnectSocket() function attempts to connect the Android to the CC3200 device over a wifi connection by doing the following:

1. Setting up a message to be printed to the debug window notifying the user that the Android is going to attempt to connect to the CC3200 device.

2. If the thread has not been frozen then update the debug window by calling the m_MainActivity.runOnUiThread() function.

3. Calling the ConnectSocket() function to perform the actual wifi connection between the Android and the CC3200. If true is returned then:

    1. Set up a message to be printed to the debug window that notifies the user that the wifi connection has been established.

    2. Create a wifi lock that prevents the Android's wifi from shutting off by calling the CreateWifiLock() function.

    3. Set m_IsConnected to true to indicate that the wifi connection has now been established.

4. Set up a message to be printed to the debug window that notifies the user that the wifi connection has been established by calling the m_MainActivity.WifiSocketConnectedMessage() function.

4. If the ConnectSocket() function returns false then setup up a message to be printed to the debug window that the connection to the CC3200 has failed.

5. If this thread is still active and not stopped then do the actual update to the debug window by calling the m_MainActivity.runOnUiThread(m_MainActivity) function.

See Listing 3-8

Listing 3-8. The CreateConnectSocket Function

```
void CreateConnectSocket()

{

        // Connect the Socket to the destination machine at IPAddress on PortNumber

        m_MainActivity.AddDebugMessageThread(TAG + ": Client Thread is Attempting to Connect to Server at '"
+ m_ServerIPAddressString + "' on port number " + m_ServerPortNumber + "\n");

        if (m_Freeze == false)

        {

                m_MainActivity.runOnUiThread(m_MainActivity);

        }


        if (ConnectSocket())

        {

                m_MainActivity.AddDebugMessageThread(TAG + ": Client Thread is Connected to Server !!!
\n");


                // Since Thread is now connected we need to lock the wifi so that it does not turn off.

                CreateWifiLock();

                m_IsConnected = true;

                m_MainActivity.WifiSocketConnectedMessage();

        }

        else

        {
```

```
                    m_MainActivity.AddDebugMessageThread(TAG + ": Client Thread FAILED to Connect to Server
!!! \n");

        }


        if (m_Freeze == false)

        {

                // Update the User Interface

                m_MainActivity.runOnUiThread(m_MainActivity);

        }

}
```

The ConnectSocket() Function

The ConnectSocket() function performs the actual wifi connection procedure of connecting the Android client thread to the CC3200 device's TCP server.

The ConnectSocket() function does the following:

1. Setting the result variable that is true if the connection was successful and false if it has failed to the default value of false.

2. Creates a new Socket object and assigns this to m_Socket

3. Retrieves the optional Socket information on the "keep alive" status by calling the m_Socket.getKeepAlive() function. With TCP the "keep alive" function is optional and defaults to false. By default TCP sockets like we are using by default do not automatically time out and disconnect. A "keep alive" message is sent between devices to maintain the connection and to make sure the connection is operating correctly. If there is an exception generated then print out an error message using the Log() function.

4. The socket created in step 1 is bound to the local host which is the Android device on any available port number by calling the m_Socket.bind(null) function with null sent as a parameter. The null value indicates that the socket should be bound to any free port on the local host. If the socket binding fails then print out error messages.

5. Retrieves the ip address of the server running on the CC3200 and assigns it to the IA variable by calling the InetAddress.getAllByName(m_ServerIPAddressString) function and referencing the first element of the returned array. The input parameter is the server ip address in string format. If there is an error in getting the ip address then error messages are output.

6. Creates a new InetSocketAddress class variable called SocketAddress that holds the socket address of that target we want to connect to which includes the ip address of the server and the port number that the TCP server is using.

7. Connects to the server by calling the m_Socket.connect(SocketAddress) function with the input parameter of the SocketAddress variable created in step 6. The m_Socket variable was created in step 2. If there is an error then error messages are printed out.

8. Retrieves the OutputStream class object that we will use to send data to the CC3200 device by calling the m_Socket.getOutputStream() function and assigning the returned value to the m_SocketOutputStream variable.

9. Retrieves the InputStream class object that we will use to read data from the CC3200 device by calling the m_Socket.getInputStream() function and assigning the returned value to the m_SocketInputStream variable.

10. If both the OutputStream and InputStream objects are successfully retrieved then the result variable is set to true. Otherwise an exception is generated and error messages are printed out.

11. The result variable is returned which indicates the success or failure of the connection attempt.

See Listing 3-9.

Listing 3-9. The ConnectSocket() Function

```
boolean ConnectSocket()

{

        boolean result = false;

        InetAddress IA = null;

        InetSocketAddress SocketAddress = null;


        // Create new socket

        m_Socket = new Socket();


        try {

                boolean keepalive = m_Socket.getKeepAlive();

                Log.e(TAG,"KeepAlive socket value = " + keepalive);

        } catch (SocketException e2) {

                // TODO Auto-generated catch block

                Log.e(TAG,"ERROR getting Keep Alive status of socket !!!");

                e2.printStackTrace();
```

```
                }


                // Bind socket to local host

                try {

                        m_Socket.bind(null);

                } catch (IOException e) {

                        Log.e(TAG,"Client Thread Socket Bind failed !!! Error = " + e.toString());

                        m_MainActivity.AddDebugMessageThread(TAG + ": Client Thread Socket Bind failed !!! Error =
" + e.toString() + "\n");

                        e.printStackTrace();

                        return result;

                }



                // Get the IP address of machine to connect to

                try {

                        IA = InetAddress.getAllByName(m_ServerIPAddressString)[0];

                } catch (UnknownHostException e1) {

                        Log.e(TAG,"Getting Server InetAddress by getAllByName() Failed ! ERROR = " + e1.toString());

                        m_MainActivity.AddDebugMessageThread(TAG + ": Getting Server InetAddress by
getAllByName() Failed ! ERROR = " + e1.toString() + "\n");

                        e1.printStackTrace();

                        return result;

                }



                // Create a new SocketAddress based on the InetAddress and port number of machine to

                // connect to.

                if (IA != null)

                {

                        SocketAddress = new InetSocketAddress(IA, m_ServerPortNumber);

                }
```

// Connect the socket to the destination machine on the port number specified by the SocketAddress object.

try {

        m_Socket.connect(SocketAddress);

} catch (IOException e) {

        Log.e(TAG,"Socket connection FAILED! ERROR = " + e.toString());

        m_MainActivity.AddDebugMessageThread(TAG + ": Socket Connection FAILED ! ERROR = " + e.toString() + "\n");

        e.printStackTrace();

        return result;

}

// Get Output and input stream from Socket for writing and reading data

try {

        m_SocketOutputStream = m_Socket.getOutputStream();

        m_SocketInputStream = m_Socket.getInputStream();

        result = true;

} catch (IOException e) {

        Log.e(TAG,"Cannot get output/input streams from socket! ERROR = " + e.toString());

        m_MainActivity.AddDebugMessageThread(TAG + ": Cannot get output/input streams from socket! ERROR = " + e.toString());

        e.printStackTrace();

        return result;

}

        return result;

}

The CreateWifiLock() Function

The CreateWifiLock() function locks the Android's wifi so that the wifi radio is always on.

The CreateWifiLock() function does the following:

1. Gets a WifiLock object from the current WifiManager by calling the m_WifiManager.createWifiLock(TAG) function with the String that will identify this particular WifiLock object in debug messages.

2. Locks the Android's wifi by calling the m_WifiLock.acquire() function.

3. If a call to the m_WifiLock.isHeld() function returns true then sets up a message to be added to the debug window that notifies the user that the wifi has been successfully locked. Otherwise, the message will notify the user that the wifi has not been successfully locked.

See Listing 3-10.

Listing 3-10. The CreateWifiLock() function

```
void CreateWifiLock()

{

        // WIFI LOCK

        m_WifiLock = m_WifiManager.createWifiLock(TAG);

        m_WifiLock.acquire();

        if (m_WifiLock.isHeld())

        {

                m_MainActivity.AddDebugMessageThread("WifiLock is aquired ..." + "\n");

        }

        else

        {

                m_MainActivity.AddDebugMessageThread("ERROR ! WifiLock aquire FAILED !!!" + "\n");

        }

}
```

The IsConnected() Function

The IsConnected() function returns true if there is a wifi connection between the Android and the CC3200 using this Client class. Otherwise, it returns false. See Listing 3-11.

Listing 3-11. The IsConnected() Function

```
boolean IsConnected()

{

        return m_IsConnected;

}
```

The Client Class Constructor

The Client class constructor initializes key class member variables with input from the MainActivity class. See Listing 3-12.

Listing 3-12. The Client constructor

```
Client(String ServerStaticIP, int PortNumber, WifiMessageHandler iWifiMessageHandler, MainActivity
iMainActivity)

{

        // Initialization

        m_MainActivity              =        iMainActivity;

        m_ServerPortNumber          =        PortNumber;

        m_WifiMessageHandler        =        iWifiMessageHandler;

        m_ServerIPAddressString     =        ServerStaticIP;

}
```

The Freeze() Function

The Freeze() function halts the execution of the class by setting m_Freeze to true and calling the m_WifiMessageHandler.Freeze() function in the wifi message handler for this class. See Listing 3-13.

Listing 3-13. The Freeze() function

```
void Freeze()

{

        m_Freeze = true;
```

```
        // Freeze WIFI Message Handler

        m_WifiMessageHandler.Freeze();

}
```

The Write() Function

The Write() function sends data in the form of bytes to the CC3200 over wifi by calling the m_SocketOutputStream.write(bytes) function with the input parameter bytes which is an array of type byte. See Listing 3-14.

Listing 3-14. The Write() function

```
public void write(byte[] bytes)

{

    try

    {

      m_SocketOutputStream.write(bytes);

    }

    catch (IOException e)

    {

        Log.e(TAG,"Error Writing Bytes to SocketOutputStream. Error = " + e.toString());

    }

}
```

The Cancel Function

The Cancel() function prepares the wifi connection to be terminated by:

1. Halting the execution of this thread by setting m_IsConnected to false indicating that the android is no longer connected to the CC3200.

2. If a wifi lock exists then release the lock by calling the m_WifiLock.release() function.

3. Close the open client connection to the TCP server on the CC3200 device by calling the m_Socket.close() function. If there is an error then print out an error message.

See Listing 3-15.

Listing 3-15. The Cancel() function

```
public void cancel()

{

        // Stop Reading from Socket

        m_IsConnected = false;


        // Release WifiLock

        if (m_WifiLock != null)

        {

                Log.e(TAG, "Releasing m_WifiLock ...");

                m_WifiLock.release();

        }


        try

        {

                // Close open client socket to TCP server

                m_Socket.close();

        }

        catch (IOException e)

        {

                Log.e(TAG,"Error closing Wifi Socket ...");

        }

}
```

The WifiMessageHandler Class

The WifiMessageHandler class processes the data returned from the CC3200 based upon the last command issued by the Android controller. The incoming data is in either text format or binary format.

Text Data

The text data format consists of numbers and letters followed by a newline character which is '\n' that indicates the end of the text data. See Figure 3-2.

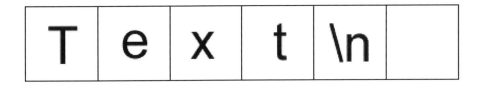

Figure 3-2. Text data

We specify the exact character to indicate the end of text using the variable m_EndData.

char   m_EndData = '\n';

The text data is read in by calling the ReceiveTextData() function

boolean ReceiveTextData(int NumberBytes, byte[] Message)

Binary Data

The binary data is a series of 1's and 0's and the length of the returned data must be known when issuing an Android command that expects binary data returned from the CC3200. See Figure 3-3.

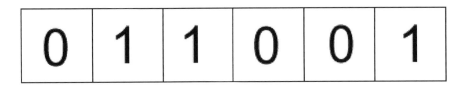

Figure 3-3. Binary Data

The data length in bytes of the incoming binary data is held in the m_DataIncomingLength variable that is declared as:

int   m_DataIncomingLength = 0;

The binary data is read in using the ReceiveBinaryData() function that is declared as follows:

boolean ReceiveBinaryData(int NumberBytes, byte[] Message)

Class Overview

The ReceiveMessage() function is the main entry point to this class and is called from the Client class. This section gives you a general overview of how this class works and how you can add your own customizations to this class.

The general procedure to handle data that is being sent from the CC3200 in response to an Android command is:

1. The Client class object calls the ReceiveMessage() function with the data received from the CC3200 and the number of bytes that data consists of.

2. The ReceiveMessage() function processes the data based on the last Android command issued to the CC3200 and calls a function ProcessXXXXCommand(NumberBytes, Message) where XXXX is replaced by the command name.

3. If the data to be received is text data then the ReceiveTextData() function is used to process the data.

4. If the data to be received is binary data then the ReceiveBinaryData() function is used to process the data.

5. Once all the text or binary data is received then you need to set a variable in the MainActivity class to indicate that the Android command has received a response from the CC3200. You do this through a command such as m_MainActivity.SetXXXXFinished() where the XXXX is replaced by the command that has just received a response from the CC3200.

6. In order to change the part of the Android user interface that the command updates you need to call m_MainActivity.runOnUiThread(m_MainActivity). This executes the run() function in the MainActivity class where the MainActivity class's user interface objects can be accessed.

See Figure 3-4.

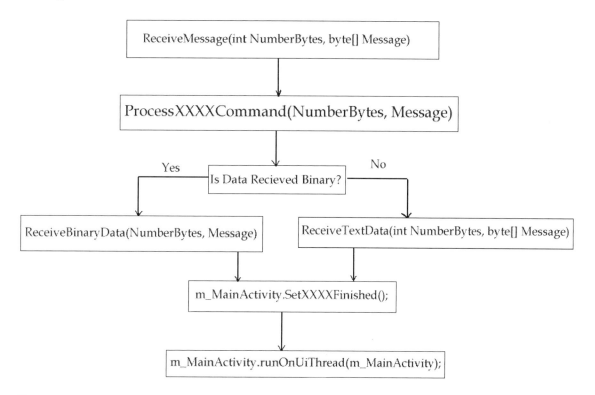

Figure 3-4. WifiMessageHandler Class flowchart

The m_Command is a String variable that holds an alphanumeric representation of the Android command that the Android expects to receive a response to. The m_Command variable is set using the SetCommand() function. See Listing 3-16.

Listing 3-16. The SetCommand() function

```
String m_Command = "";

void SetCommand(String Command)

{

        m_Command = Command;

}
```

The m_MainActivity variable holds a reference to the MainActivity class object that created this WlfiMessageHandler object.

```
MainActivity m_MainActivity;
```

The m_USAscii variable holds the character set to use when converting incoming bytes into alphanumeric text.

```
Charset   m_USAscii   = null;
```

The m_Data variable holds text data

```
String    m_Data    = "";
```

The m_DataIncomingLength variable holds the length in bytes of the data expected to be sent by the CC3200.

```
int       m_DataIncomingLength = 0;
```

The m_DataByte array is an array of bytes of size m_DataSize that holds the binary data that will be sent by the CC3200.

```
byte[]    m_DataByte = new byte[m_DataSize];
```

The m_DataSize variable holds the size of the binary data buffer used to store incoming binary data and is set to 700,000 bytes long.

```
int       m_DataSize = 700000;
```

The m_DataIndex variable holds the index into the m_DataByte array and indicates the next available empty position in the array that can hold a new value.

```
int     m_DataIndex = 0;
```

The SetDataReceiveLength() function is called from the MainActivity class and sets the length of the expected incoming binary data in bytes.

```
void SetDataReceiveLength(int length) { m_DataIncomingLength = length;}
```

The GetBinaryData() function returns a reference to m_DataByte which holds binary data sent from the CC3200.

byte[] GetBinaryData(){return m_DataByte;}

The GetBinaryDataLength() function returns the length in bytes of the data in the m_DataByte array.

int GetBinaryDataLength() { return m_DataIndex;}

The m_Freeze variable is true if the Client thread that calls this class has been halted and false otherwise. The volatile modifier on this variable means that that value can be changed from another thread.

volatile boolean m_Freeze = false;

The Freeze() function sets the m_Freeze variable to true which halts this class from processing any more incoming data from the CC3200.

void Freeze() {m_Freeze = true;}

The GetStringData() function

The GetStringData() function returns the text data sent from the CC3200 that is stored in m_Data. The m_Data variable is also reset to the null string. See Listing 3-17.

Listing 3-17. GetStringData() function

```
// Get String Data and resets internal String Data variable

String GetStringData()

{

    String temp = m_Data;

    m_Data = "";


    return temp;

}
```

The ResetData() function

The ResetData() function initializes the text and binary data structures that are used to receive data from the CC3200 by:

1. Setting m_Data which holds the incoming text data to "".

2. Setting m_DataIndex that holds the position of the next available byte in the incoming binary data buffer to 0 that is the beginning of the buffer.

3. Setting m_DataIncomingLength that holds the length in bytes of the expected binary data from CC3200 to 0.

4. Erasing the existing data in the binary data buffer m_DataByte by writing 0 to every array location.

See Listing 3-18.

Listing 3-18. The ResetData() function

```
void ResetData()

{

    // Reset String Data

    m_Data = "";


    // Reset Binary Data

    m_DataIndex = 0;

    m_DataIncomingLength = 0;


    // Erase old data in array

    for (int i = 0 ; i < m_DataSize; i++)

    {

            m_DataByte[i] = 0;

    }

}
```

The WifiMessageHandler Class Constructor

The class constructor initializes the class object by:

1. Assigning the global variable m_MainActivity to the Actvity class object that will use this handler.

2. Assigns the US ASCII character set to m_USAscii by calling Charset.forName("US-ASCII"). The m_USAscii variable is used to convert incoming text data into US English characters.

See Listing 3-19.

Listing 3-19. The Constructor

```
WifiMessageHandler(MainActivity iActivity)

{

    m_MainActivity = iActivity;


    // Set Charset to US ASCII translation

    m_USAscii = Charset.forName("US-ASCII");

}
```

The ReceiveTextData() function

The ReceiveTextData() function reads in the data from the Message byte array input parameter and returns true if a complete text data message has been received and false otherwise.

Specifically, the function does the following:

1. Read in the valid data from the Message array based on the NumberBytes input parameter.

2. Convert this data into a ByteBuffer object using the ByteBuffer.wrap(temp) function with temp being the valid data from Step 1.

3. Convert the ByteBuffer object into a CharBuffer object by calling the m_USAscii.decode(bb) function with the input parameter bb being the ByteBuffer obtained in Step 2.

4. Convert the CharBuffer object obtained in the previous step into a String object by calling the TempCharBuffer.toString() function on the CharBuffer object.

5. Add the String obtained from Step 4 to the current text data message which is stored in m_Data.

6. Next, we check to see if the end of the text message has been reached. We first find the array index value of the text end message character that is stored in m_EndData by calling the m_Data.indexOf(m_EndData) function.

7. If the returned value is greater than or equal to 0 then we have found the end of text message marker and this text message is complete.

See Listing 3-20.

Listing 3- 20. The ReceiveTextData() function

```
boolean ReceiveTextData(int NumberBytes, byte[] Message)

{

    boolean EndTextDataFound = false;
```

```java
        byte[] temp = new byte[NumberBytes];


        // Capture readable data

        for (int i = 0; i < NumberBytes; i++)

        {

                temp[i] = Message[i];

        }

        ByteBuffer bb = ByteBuffer.wrap(temp);


        // Convert from bytes to printable characters

        CharBuffer TempCharBuffer = m_USAscii.decode(bb);


        // Debug output Number of bytes incoming and characters

        m_Message = TempCharBuffer.toString();

        Log.d("ZombieCopter Text Recieve NumberBytes " , NumberBytes + "");

        Log.d("ZombieCopter Text Recieve Partial Message",  m_Message);


        // Add Partial Message to Complete Data

        m_Data += m_Message;


        // Check if end of data has been reached

        int EndOfData = m_Data.indexOf(m_EndData);

        if (EndOfData >= 0)

        {

                // All Text Data Has been Read in

                EndTextDataFound = true;

        }

        return EndTextDataFound;

    }
```

The ReceiveBinaryData() function

The ReceiveBinaryData() function reads in the incoming binary data from the CC3200.

The function does the following:

1. Reads in the incoming binary data from the Message byte array and stores it in the m_DataByte array. The m_DataIndex variable that indicates the next empty position in the m_DataByte array, is incremented.

2. If m_DataIndex is greater than or equal to the expected length of the incoming binary message which is held in m_DataIncomingLength then the incoming binary message has completed. Otherwise, more data needs to be read in from the CC3200.

See Listing 3-21.

Listing 3-21. The ReceiveBinaryData() function

```
boolean ReceiveBinaryData(int NumberBytes, byte[] Message)

{

        boolean Finished = false;


        // Add incoming Binary data to bytes data array

        for (int i = 0; i < NumberBytes; i++)

        {

                m_DataByte[m_DataIndex] = Message[i];

                m_DataIndex++;

        }


        // Check to see if all binary data has been received

        if (m_DataIndex >= m_DataIncomingLength)

        {

                Finished = true;

        }

        return Finished;

}
```

The ReceiveMessage() function

The ReceiveMessage() function is called whenever data from the CC3200 is received by the Android using wifi.

The function does the following:

1. If m_Freeze = true then do not process any further input from the CC3200.

2. If the Android command that is waiting on a response from the CC3200 is "GetImageSize" then process the command by calling the ProcessGetImageSizeCommand(NumberBytes, Message) function with the parameters Message which contains an array of bytes from the CC3200 and NumberBytes which contains the number of valid bytes in the array. This command retrieves the size of the image that was just taken and the size is in text format.

3. If the Android command is "GetImageData" then process the incoming data by calling the ProcessGetImageDataCommand(NumberBytes, Message) function which reads in the image data from the CC3200.

4. If the Android command is "GetTextData" then call the ProcessReceiveTextDataCommand(NumberBytes, Message) function. This command is not used but serves as an example of how you can expand this program to add commands that do other things.

5. If m_Command which is the Android command that is waiting on a response from the CC3200 does not match any of the above then print out an error message by calling the Log() function.

See Listing 3-22.

Listing 3-22. The ReceiveMessage() Function

```
void ReceiveMessage(int NumberBytes, byte[] Message)

{

        // Check to see if this thread has been frozen by the main activity thread

        if (m_Freeze == true)

        {

                return;

        }


        // Process Incoming Data

        // Assume incoming data is associated with the current m_Command variable

        // and process the Message accordingly.

        if (m_Command == "GetImageSize")
```

```
            {

                    ProcessGetImageSizeCommand(NumberBytes, Message);

            }

            else

            if (m_Command == "GetImageData")

            {

                    ProcessGetImageDataCommand(NumberBytes, Message);

            }

            else

            if (m_Command == "GetTextData")

            {

                    ProcessReceiveTextDataCommand(NumberBytes, Message);

            }

            else

            {

                    Log.e("WIFI Handler" , "Error - Command for Data Receive Not Found!!!!!!");

            }

    }
```

The ProcessGetImageSizeCommand() Function

The ProcessGetImageSizeCommand() processes the size of the image that was just captured by the CC3200's camera.

The ProcessGetImageSizeCommand() function does the following:

1. Reads in incoming data assuming that the data is a text string and is terminated by the character held in m_EndData by calling the ReceiveTextData(NumberBytes, Message) function.

2. If the incoming data has all been read in then:

    1. If this thread has not been halted then continue execution of this function

    2. Set up the MainActivity's user interface to be updated by calling the m_MainActivity.TakePhotoCommandCallback() function.

3. The MainActivity's user interface is actually updated by calling the
    m_MainActivity.runOnUiThread(m_MainActivity) function which executes the MainActivity
    class's run() function.

See Listing 3-23.

Listing 3-23. The ProcessGetImageSizeCommand() Function

```
void ProcessGetImageSizeCommand(int NumberBytes, byte[] Message)

{

        boolean FinishedReceivingText = ReceiveTextData(NumberBytes, Message);

        if (FinishedReceivingText)

        {

                if (m_Freeze == false)

                {

                        // Process Remote Directory Command

                        m_MainActivity.TakePhotoCommandCallback();


                        // Update the User Interface

                        m_MainActivity.runOnUiThread(m_MainActivity);

                }

        }

}
```

The ProcessGetImageDataCommand() Function

The ProcessGetImageDataCommand() function processes the actual incoming image data that
was taken by the camera.

The ProcessGetImageDataCommand() function does the following:

1. Starts to receive the incoming binary data from the CC3200 by calling the
    ReceiveBinaryData(NumberBytes, Message) function.

2. If the binary data has finished being read in and the client thread has not been halted then set
    up the MainActivity class to process the data by calling the
    m_MainActivity.TakePhotoCommandCallback() function.

3. Perform the actual update to the MainActivity's user interface by calling the m_MainActivity.runOnUiThread(m_MainActivity) function.

See Listing 3-24.

Listing 3-24. The ProcessGetImageDataCommand() function

```
void ProcessGetImageDataCommand(int NumberBytes, byte[] Message)

{

        boolean FinishedReceivingData = ReceiveBinaryData(NumberBytes, Message);

        if (FinishedReceivingData)

        {

                if (m_Freeze == false)

                {

                        // Process Take Picture Command

                        m_MainActivity.TakePhotoCommandCallback();


                        // Update the User Interface

                        m_MainActivity.runOnUiThread(m_MainActivity);

                }

        }

}
```

The ProcessReceiveTextDataCommand() Function

The ProcessReceiveTextDataCommand() function processes incoming text data from the CC3200 and is not used but illustrates how you can read in generic text data from the CC3200 and have it processed by the MainActivity class.

The function does the following:

1. Reads in text data from the CC3200 by calling the ReceiveTextData(NumberBytes, Message) function.

2. If all the text data has been read in and the execution of this class has not been halted then prepare the MainActivity's user interface to be updated by calling the m_MainActivity.SetRecieveTextDataCallbackFinished() function.

3. The actual update in the MainActivity class using the newly read in text data is done by calling the m_MainActivity.runOnUiThread(m_MainActivity) function which calls the MainActivity class's run() function.

See Listing 3-25.

Listing 3-25. The ProcessReceiveTextDataCommand() function

```
void ProcessReceiveTextDataCommand(int NumberBytes, byte[] Message)

{

        boolean FinishedReceivingText = ReceiveTextData(NumberBytes, Message);

        if (FinishedReceivingText)

        {

            if (m_Freeze == false)

            {

                // Process Receive Text Data Command

                m_MainActivity.SetRecieveTextDataCallbackFinished();


                // Update the User Interface

                m_MainActivity.runOnUiThread(m_MainActivity);

            }

        }

}
```

Cleaning Up Wifi on Application Exit

In terms of cleaning up the wifi connection on application exit we put the code to terminate the Android's wifi connection in the MainActivity class in the onDestroy() function. The onDestroy() function is called when the Android application is destroyed on application exit.

The wifi connection is terminated in the onDestroy() function by:

1. If the Android client is connected to the CC3200 then send a terminate command to the CC3200 by calling the SendTerminateServerCommand() function. Next, cancel the thread by calling the m_ClientConnectThread.cancel() function.

2. If the Android client is not connected then halt its execution by calling the m_ClientConnectThread.Freeze() function.

3. Turn off the Android's wifi by calling the
    m_ClientConnectThread.m_WifiManager.setWifiEnabled(false) function with the false parameter.

4. Set the reference count of the Client object to 0 by assigning "null" to the
    m_ClientConnectThread variable which points to the Client object. This tells the Android operating
    system that the Client thread is no longer being used and can be killed.

See Listing 3-26.

Listing 3-26. The onDestroy() function

```
@Override

protected void onDestroy()

{

        Log.e(TAG, "In onDestroy() FUNCTION !!!!!!!!");

        super.onDestroy();


        // Stop playing sound effects

        StopSounds();


        // Shutdown Text To Speech

        m_TTS.shutdown();


        // Shutdown Client Thread to Server

        if (m_ClientConnectThread != null)

        {

                if (m_ClientConnectThread.IsConnected())

                {

                        // Terminate TDP Server running on CC3200

                        SendTerminateServerCommand();


                        // Close Client Thread

                        Log.e(TAG, "Cancelling Client Connect Thread!!!!!!!!");
```

```
                m_ClientConnectThread.cancel();

        }

        else

        {

                // Thread not connected to server so freeze its execution

                m_ClientConnectThread.Freeze();

        }

    }


    // Turn off Wifi

    m_ClientConnectThread.m_WifiManager.setWifiEnabled(false);


    // Discard Thread

    m_ClientConnectThread = null;

}
```

The SendTerminateServerCommand() Function

The SendTerminateServerCommand() function sends a "terminate" command to the CC3200 device which stops and then restarts the TCP server. See Listing 3-27.

Listing 3-27. The SendTerminateServerCommand() function

```
void SendTerminateServerCommand()

{

        String Command = "terminate";


        // Set Up Data Handler

        m_WifiMessageHandler.ResetData();

        m_WifiMessageHandler.SetCommand("terminate");


        if (m_ClientConnectThread != null)
```

```
    {
        if (m_ClientConnectThread.IsConnected())

        {
                m_TakePhotoButton.setEnabled(false);

                m_ClientConnectThread.write(Command.getBytes());

                Log.e(TAG, "Sending terminate command to TCP Server ...");

        }

    }

}
```

Summary

In this chapter I covered the Android controller and the Android's wifi that is used to connect to the CC3200 device. I first cover how you can get started developing programs for the Android operating system by covering the official Android Studio IDE and the older Android ADT Bundle IDE. Next, I discuss the Java programming language that will be used for developing Android programs. Basic Java data types and basic concepts are reviewed. I next present how an Android device can establish a wifi connection with a CC3200 device. I cover the Client class which is used to connect the Android device to the CC3200 device. Finally, I cover the WifiMessageHandler class which handles the incoming data from the CC3200 device.

Chapter 4

The CC3200 and Wifi Communication

In this chapter I cover how to use the wifi on a CC3200 device that is in access point mode. The CC3200 will be running a TCP server that processes incoming commands from the Android client device. I first cover the available wifi network modes available on the CC3200. Next, I show you how to put the CC3200 device into the default state. Then, I cover how to put the CC3200 into access point mode. Setting up a static ip address on the CC3200 device is then covered. Next, I discuss how to create a TCP server that will process incoming Android camera commands. Finally, I show you how the TCP server is restarted after the Android "terminate" command is sent.

Overview of Wifi Network Modes on the CC3200

The CC3200 can be operated in three different modes which are:

- Wifi Station Mode which is used to connect the CC3200 to your local wifi network.

- Wifi Access Point Mode which makes your CC3200 device an access point where other devices such as an Android phone can connect to it.

- Wifi P2P or Peer to Peer Mode which is a wifi networking method where many devices can be connected to one another in their own private network without using an access point.

The Access Point or AP mode of the CC3200 is what we will use in this book to develop the security system. The Android device will connect to the CC3200 that is running in access point or AP mode.

Setting the CC3200 to the Default State

The first thing you need to do before setting up the CC3200 into AP mode is to set the CC3200 into the default station mode. The function that does this is called the ConfigureSimpleLinkToDefaultState() function.

The ConfigureSimpleLinkToDefaultState() function does the following:

1. Start up and initialize the wifi system on the CC3200 by calling the sl_Start() function. The return value is stored in the lMode variable.

2. Check the return value from the sl_Start() function called in step 1 by executing ASSERT_ON_ERROR(lMode) which is a macro that prints out an error message to the UART and Terra Term if the returned value is less than 0. The macro calls the Report() function to actually print out the error.

3. If the CC3200 is not in station mode but is in AP mode then wait until an IP address has been acquired before continuing execution.

4. Sets the CC3200 into station mode by calling the sl_WlanSetMode(ROLE_STA) function with the ROLE_STA parameter that sets the CC3200 into station mode. The return value is assigned to the lRetVal variable.

5. Checks for and prints out any errors if they occur to the UART which is read by the Terra Term program by calling the ASSERT_ON_ERROR(lRetVal) function with the return value from step 4 as a parameter.

6. Shuts down the Simplelink device and wifi by calling the sl_Stop(0xFF) function. The device waits for up to 0xFF milliseconds before hibernating. If an error is returned then it is processed and displayed through the UART and Terra Term.

7. Start up the CC3200 Simplelink system by calling the sl_Start(0, 0, 0) function. If an error occurs then display this error though the UART.

8. If the returned value from step 7 indicates that the CC3200 is not in station mode then exit the function and return a DEVICE_NOT_IN_STATION_MODE value. This means that there could be a hardware failure and that your CC3200 device is not working properly.

9. Retrieve the device configuration of the CC3200 by calling the sl_DevGet() function and displays any errors that may occur using the UART.

10. Print out key information about the CC3200 such as the host driver version and build version by calling the UART_PRINT() functions. Information retrieved in step 9 is also used.

11. Configures the wifi connection policy to auto and autosmartconfig.

12. Delete all the wireless local area network (WLAN) profiles by calling the sl_WlanProfileDel(0xFF) function with the 0xFF parameter which indicates that all the profiles on the CC3200 device are to be erased.

13. Disconnect the CC3200 from any wireless network it may be part of by calling the sl_WlanDisconnect() function.

14. Enable the DHCP client by calling the sl_NetCfgSet() function. DHCP stands for dynamic host configuration protocol which assigns ip addresses to hosts on demand as well as other configuration items such as the subnet mask and the gateway.

15. Disables the wifi scan policy by calling the sl_WlanPolicySet() function.

16. Sets the wifi transmission power for station mode to full power by calling the sl_WlanSet(SL_WLAN_CFG_GENERAL_PARAM_ID,WLAN_GENERAL_PARAM_OPT_STA_TX_POWER, 1, (unsigned char *)&ucPower) function. The

WLAN_GENERAL_PARAM_OPT_STA_TX_POWER parameter sets the wifi transmission power level and the ucPower parameter is 0 that means full power.

17. Sets the power management of the device to normal or default mode by calling the sl_WlanPolicySet(SL_POLICY_PM , SL_NORMAL_POLICY, NULL, 0) function. The SL_POLICY_PM parameter specifies that this will set the policy for the power management system. The SL_NORMAL_POLICY specifies normal or default power management.

18. The mDNS service is deleted from the mDNS package and the database by calling the sl_NetAppMDNSUnRegisterService(0, 0) function.

19. Removes all the filters by calling the sl_WlanRxFilterSet() function with SL_REMOVE_RX_FILTER as the first parameter.

20. Stops the Simplelink device and any wifi activity that may be happening by calling the sl_Stop(SL_STOP_TIMEOUT) function with the timeout value SL_STOP_TIMEOUT.

21. Initialize the variables for the CC3200 application by calling the InitializeAppVariables() function.

See Listing 4-1.

Listing 4-1. The ConfigureSimpleLinkToDefaultState() function

```
static long ConfigureSimpleLinkToDefaultState()

{

    SlVersionFull   ver = {0};

    _WlanRxFilterOperationCommandBuff_t RxFilterIdMask = {0};


    unsigned char ucVal = 1;

    unsigned char ucConfigOpt = 0;

    unsigned char ucConfigLen = 0;

    unsigned char ucPower = 0;


    long lRetVal = -1;

    long lMode = -1;


    lMode = sl_Start(0, 0, 0);

    ASSERT_ON_ERROR(lMode);
```

```
    // If the device is not in station-mode, try configuring it in station-mode

    if (ROLE_STA != lMode)

    {

        if (ROLE_AP == lMode)

        {

            // If the device is in AP mode, we need to wait for this event

            // before doing anything

            while(!IS_IP_ACQUIRED(g_ulStatus))

            {
#ifndef SL_PLATFORM_MULTI_THREADED

                _SlNonOsMainLoopTask();

#endif

            }

        }


        // Switch to STA role and restart

        lRetVal = sl_WlanSetMode(ROLE_STA);

        ASSERT_ON_ERROR(lRetVal);


        lRetVal = sl_Stop(0xFF);

        ASSERT_ON_ERROR(lRetVal);


        lRetVal = sl_Start(0, 0, 0);

        ASSERT_ON_ERROR(lRetVal);


        // Check if the device is in station again

        if (ROLE_STA != lRetVal)

        {
```

```
    // We don't want to proceed if the device is not coming up in STA-mode

    return DEVICE_NOT_IN_STATION_MODE;

  }

}


// Get the device's version-information

ucConfigOpt = SL_DEVICE_GENERAL_VERSION;

ucConfigLen = sizeof(ver);

lRetVal = sl_DevGet(SL_DEVICE_GENERAL_CONFIGURATION, &ucConfigOpt,

               &ucConfigLen, (unsigned char *)(&ver));

ASSERT_ON_ERROR(lRetVal);


UART_PRINT("Host Driver Version: %s\n\r",SL_DRIVER_VERSION);

UART_PRINT("Build Version %d.%d.%d.%d.31.%d.%d.%d.%d.%d.%d.%d.%d\n\r",

ver.NwpVersion[0],ver.NwpVersion[1],ver.NwpVersion[2],ver.NwpVersion[3],

ver.ChipFwAndPhyVersion.FwVersion[0],ver.ChipFwAndPhyVersion.FwVersion[1],

ver.ChipFwAndPhyVersion.FwVersion[2],ver.ChipFwAndPhyVersion.FwVersion[3],

ver.ChipFwAndPhyVersion.PhyVersion[0],ver.ChipFwAndPhyVersion.PhyVersion[1],

ver.ChipFwAndPhyVersion.PhyVersion[2],ver.ChipFwAndPhyVersion.PhyVersion[3]);


// Set connection policy to Auto + SmartConfig

//    (Device's default connection policy)

lRetVal = sl_WlanPolicySet(SL_POLICY_CONNECTION,

                SL_CONNECTION_POLICY(1, 0, 0, 0, 1), NULL, 0);

ASSERT_ON_ERROR(lRetVal);


// Remove all profiles

lRetVal = sl_WlanProfileDel(0xFF);

ASSERT_ON_ERROR(lRetVal);
```

```
    //

    // Device in station-mode. Disconnect previous connection if any

    // The function returns 0 if 'Disconnected done', negative number if already

    // disconnected Wait for 'disconnection' event if 0 is returned, Ignore

    // other return-codes

    //

    lRetVal = sl_WlanDisconnect();

    if(0 == lRetVal)

    {

        // Wait

        while(IS_CONNECTED(g_ulStatus))

        {

#ifndef SL_PLATFORM_MULTI_THREADED

            _SlNonOsMainLoopTask();

#endif

        }

    }


    // Enable DHCP client

    lRetVal = sl_NetCfgSet(SL_IPV4_STA_P2P_CL_DHCP_ENABLE,1,1,&ucVal);

    ASSERT_ON_ERROR(lRetVal);


    // Disable scan

    ucConfigOpt = SL_SCAN_POLICY(0);

    lRetVal = sl_WlanPolicySet(SL_POLICY_SCAN , ucConfigOpt, NULL, 0);

    ASSERT_ON_ERROR(lRetVal);


    // Set Tx power level for station mode
```

```
// Number between 0-15, as dB offset from max power - 0 will set max power

ucPower = 0;

lRetVal = sl_WlanSet(SL_WLAN_CFG_GENERAL_PARAM_ID,

                WLAN_GENERAL_PARAM_OPT_STA_TX_POWER,

                1,

                (unsigned char *)&ucPower);

ASSERT_ON_ERROR(lRetVal);


// Set PM policy to normal

lRetVal = sl_WlanPolicySet(SL_POLICY_PM , SL_NORMAL_POLICY, NULL, 0);

ASSERT_ON_ERROR(lRetVal);


// Unregister mDNS services

lRetVal = sl_NetAppMDNSUnRegisterService(0, 0);

ASSERT_ON_ERROR(lRetVal);


// Remove  all 64 filters (8*8)

memset(RxFilterIdMask.FilterIdMask, 0xFF, 8);

lRetVal = sl_WlanRxFilterSet(SL_REMOVE_RX_FILTER, (_u8 *)&RxFilterIdMask,

        sizeof(_WlanRxFilterOperationCommandBuff_t));

ASSERT_ON_ERROR(lRetVal);


lRetVal = sl_Stop(SL_STOP_TIMEOUT);

ASSERT_ON_ERROR(lRetVal);


InitializeAppVariables();


return lRetVal; // Success

}
```

Setting up a CC3200 Access Point

The access point on the CC3200 is set up in the ConfigureMode() function.

The ConfigureMode() function does the following:

1. Set mode for the CC3200 to access point mode by calling the sl_WlanSetMode(ROLE_AP) function with ROLE_AP as a parameter.

2. The name of the access point is set by calling the sl_WlanSet(SL_WLAN_CFG_AP_ID, WLAN_AP_OPT_SSID, strlen(AP_NAME),(unsigned char*)AP_NAME) function. The SL_WLAN_CFG_AP_ID parameter indicates that a configuration parameter relating to the access point mode of the CC3200 will be set. The WLAN_AP_OPT_SSID parameter indicates that the SSID will be set. The strlen(AP_NAME) parameter is the length of the SSID name that is being set. Finally, the AP_NAME holds the actual name of the SSID being set.

3. A debug message is printed to the UART by calling the UART_PRINT("Device is configured in AP mode\n\r") function. This message notifies the user that the CC3200 has now been configured in access point mode.

4. The Simplelink wifi processor is stopped by calling the sl_Stop(SL_STOP_TIMEOUT) function. The parameter SL_STOP_TIMEOUT is the maximum time to wait for a response from the device before going into hibernation mode.

5. Clear the status bits in the g_ulStatus variable by calling the CLR_STATUS_BIT_ALL(g_ulStatus) macro which sets g_ulStatus to 0.

6. Start the Simplelink device by calling the sl_Start(NULL,NULL,NULL) function. The CC3200 device should now be in access point mode.

See Listing 4-2.

Listing 4-2. The ConfigureMode() function

```
static int ConfigureMode(int iMode)

{

  long  lRetVal = -1;


  lRetVal = sl_WlanSetMode(ROLE_AP);

  ASSERT_ON_ERROR(lRetVal);


  // Rob's

  lRetVal = sl_WlanSet(SL_WLAN_CFG_AP_ID,

                WLAN_AP_OPT_SSID,
```

```
                        strlen(AP_NAME),

                        (unsigned char*)AP_NAME);

        ASSERT_ON_ERROR(lRetVal);


        UART_PRINT("Device is configured in AP mode\n\r");


        /* Restart Network processor */

        lRetVal = sl_Stop(SL_STOP_TIMEOUT);


        // reset status bits

        CLR_STATUS_BIT_ALL(g_ulStatus);


        return sl_Start(NULL,NULL,NULL);

}
```

Setting up a Static IP on the CC3200

The SetStaticIP() function sets the IP address of the CC3200 and does the following:

1. The static ip is set on the CC3200 by calling the
    sl_NetCfgSet(SL_IPV4_AP_P2P_GO_STATIC_ENABLE,
    IPCONFIG_MODE_ENABLE_IPV4, sizeof(SlNetCfgIpV4Args_t), (_u8 *)&ipV4) function. The
    first parameter enables the static ip feature for the access point. The second parameter
    enables the IPV4 method of specifying an ip address which is four numbers such as
    128.0.0.1. The third parameter is the size of the structure that specifies the static ip and
    related information. The final parameter is the actual structure variable that holds the static ip
    information. The actual static IP information is:

    - The ip address of the CC3200 is set to 10.1.1.1

    - The subnet mask is set to 255.255.255.0

    - The default gateway is set to 10.1.1.1

    - The DNS server address is set to 10.1.1.1

2. If the return value is less than zero which indicates an error then print out a debug
    message to the UART that there is an error. Otherwise print out a message
    indicating that the static ip was successfully set.

3. The Simplelink device sets the network configuration parameters for the DHCP (Dynamic Host Configuration Protocol) by calling the sl_NetAppSet(SL_NET_APP_DHCP_SERVER_ID, NETAPP_SET_DHCP_SRV_BASIC_OPT, sizeof(SlNetAppDhcpServerBasicOpt_t), (_u8*)&dhcpParams) function. The first parameter indicates that a configuration involving the DHCP server will be set. The second parameter indicates that the basic options of the DHCP server will be set. The third parameter is the size of the structure to be input. The last parameter is the structure that contains the configuration parameters to change. The parameters that are set in the DHCP are the following:

- The lease time is set to 1000

- The start of the ip address range for DHCP is set to 10.1.1.10

- The end of the ip address range for the DHCP is set to 10.1.1.255

4. The success or failure of the DHCP configuration attempt will be printed to the UART using the Report() function.

5. The CC3200's Simplelink system is shut down by calling the sl_Stop(0) function.

6. The CC3200's Simplelink system is turned back on by calling the sl_Start(NULL,NULL,NULL) function.

7. A message is printed out to the UART using the Report() function on the success or failure of the sl_Start() function.

See Listing 4-3

Listing 4-3. The SetStaticIP(0 function

```
void SetStaticIP()

{

        //SL_IPV4_AP_P2P_GO_STATIC_ENABLE:

        //Setting a static IP address to the device working in AP mode or P2P go.

        //The IP address will be stored in the FileSystem. Requires restart.


        SlNetCfgIpV4Args_t ipV4;

        long lRetVal = 0;


        /////////////////////////////// Set Static IP

        // Static IP - 10.1.1.1
```

```
ipV4.ipV4 =(_u32)SL_IPV4_VAL(10,1,1,1);              // _u32 IP address

ipV4.ipV4Mask = (_u32)SL_IPV4_VAL(255,255,255,0);   // _u32 Subnet mask for this AP/P2P

ipV4.ipV4Gateway = (_u32)SL_IPV4_VAL(10,1,1,1);      // _u32 Default gateway address

ipV4.ipV4DnsServer = (_u32)SL_IPV4_VAL(10,1,1,1);    // _u32 DNS server address


lRetVal = sl_NetCfgSet(SL_IPV4_AP_P2P_GO_STATIC_ENABLE,

                    IPCONFIG_MODE_ENABLE_IPV4,

                    sizeof(SlNetCfgIpV4Args_t),

                    (_u8 *)&ipV4);

if (lRetVal < 0)

{

        Report("ERROR CC3200 Static IP Can Not Be Set !!!\n\r");

}

else

{

        Report("CC3200 Static IP Set ok ...\n\r");

}


///////////////////////// Set DHCP, needed because IP is changed

SlNetAppDhcpServerBasicOpt_t dhcpParams = {0};


// Static IP - 10.1.1.1

dhcpParams.lease_time    = 1000;


//IP_LEASE_TIME;

dhcpParams.ipv4_addr_start = (_u32)SL_IPV4_VAL(10,1,1,10);   //DHCP_START_IP;

dhcpParams.ipv4_addr_last  = (_u32)SL_IPV4_VAL(10,1,1,255); //DHCP_END_IP;


lRetVal = sl_NetAppSet(SL_NET_APP_DHCP_SERVER_ID,
```

```
                    NETAPP_SET_DHCP_SRV_BASIC_OPT,

                    sizeof(SlNetAppDhcpServerBasicOpt_t),

                    ( u8*)&dhcpParams);

        if (lRetVal < 0)

        {

                Report("ERROR CC3200 NEW DHCP Can Not Be Set !!!\n\r");

        }

        else

        {

                Report("CC3200 NEW DHCP Set ok ...\n\r");

        }


        sl_Stop(0);

        lRetVal = sl_Start(NULL,NULL,NULL);

        if (lRetVal < 0)

        {

                Report("Restart Error after Static IP Set !!!\n\r");

        }

        else

        {

                Report("Restart from CC3200 Static IP Set ok ...\n\r");

        }

}
```

Creating a TCP Server on the CC3200

The TCP server that runs on the CC3200 is responsible for reading incoming commands from the Android device, processing them, and sending out the requested data over the wifi connection.

The variable that holds the incoming data that is read in from the Android is the uBuf variable. The buffer itself is a character array of 1400 bytes and is called BsdBuf.

```
#define BUF_SIZE 1400
```

```
union

{

    char BsdBuf[BUF_SIZE];

} uBuf;
```

The available camera resolutions are QQVGA, QVGA, and VGA which are enumerated types called CameraResolution.

```
typedef enum

{

        QQVGA,

        QVGA,

        VGA

}CameraResolution;
```

The variable that keeps track of the current camera resolution is called g_CameraResolution and is set by default to QVGA.

```
CameraResolution g_CameraResolution = QVGA;
```

The g_CameraInit variable is 0 if the camera has not yet been initialized and 1 if it has been initialized.

```
int g_CameraInit = 0;
```

The BsdTcpServer() function does the following:

1. The uBuf.BsdBuf array is initialized.

2. Initialize the LocalAddr variable which is used in the creation of the server socket by:

    1. Setting the LocalAddr.sin_family variable to SL_AF_INET. This sets the server socket to an IPv4 type of socket which uses 4 bytes and is in the form of four numbers such as 128.0.0.0.

    2. The format of the Port input parameter is converted from processor order to network order by using the sl_Htons((unsigned short)Port) function with Port as the input parameter. What this does is reverse the order of the bytes in the number so that the least significant byte is now the most significant byte in the number and the most significant byte is now the least significant byte in the number. The result is assigned to LocalAddr.sin_port.

    3. The LocalAddr.sin_addr.s_addr field is set to 0.

3. A new socket is created by calling the sl_Socket(SL_AF_INET,SL_SOCK_STREAM, 0) function. The first parameter indicates that this socket will be from the IPv4 protocol family

with 4 bytes and 4 numbers specifying an internet address. The second parameter indicates that the connection will be a socket stream. The final parameter which is 0 indicates that the default transport type will be used. The new socket is assigned to the SockID variable.

4. Print out the result of the socket creation in step 3 to the UART by using the Report() function.

5. Calculate the size of the SlSockAddrIn_t structure and assign the returned value to AddrSize.

6. A name is assigned to the SockID handle created in step 3 by calling the sl_Bind(SockID, (SlSockAddr_t *)&LocalAddr, AddrSize) function. The first parameter is the socket handle. The second parameter is the address for the socket, and the last parameter is the size of the address.

7. If the bind operation fails then call the sl_Close(SockID) function with the socket handle to close the socket and release system resources allocated to the socket. Print out the error or success to the UART.

8. Listen for connections to a socket by calling the sl_Listen(SockID, 0) function. The first parameter is the handle of the socket to listen to which is SockID that was created in step 3. The second parameter specifies the maximum length of the queue for pending connections for this socket and is set to 0.

9. If there was an error generated then close the socket by calling the sl_Close(SockID). Print out the results to the UART.

10. Set the server socket which is SockID to nonblocking by calling the sl_SetSockOpt(SockID, SL_SOL_SOCKET, SL_SO_NONBLOCKING,&nonBlocking, sizeof(nonBlocking)) function. Nonblocking means that the CC3200 program will not wait for a connection when the sl_Accept() function is called. Blocking means that the sl_Accept() function will wait or block until there is a connection before continuing program execution. The first parameter is the socket handle that options will be altered for. The second parameter indicates that the options will be changed at the socket level. The third parameter sets the socket option to change. The fourth parameter is the address of the variable that is set to 1 which indicates that non blocking is true or enabled. The last parameter is the size of the variable in the previous parameter.

11. The failure or success of the operation is printed out to the UART.

12. The newSockID variable is set to SL_EAGAIN. This is an error which means "try again". For a non blocking socket if the sl_Accept() function does not connect to a remote device then this error is returned meaning that you will need to "try again" to make a connection.

13. While there is no connection to the server socket and the CC3200 has an ip address acquired do the following:

    1. Accept a connection on the SockID server socket by calling the sl_Accept(SockID, (struct SlSockAddr_t *)&Addr, (SlSocklen_t*)&AddrSize) function. The first parameter is the handle of the server socket. The second parameter is a SlSockAddr_t structure that returns the address of a newly created peer socket. The last parameter is the size of the address returned in the previous parameter. The return value from this function is assigned to newSockID.

    2. If the newSockID has the value of SL_EAGAIN then wait for 1 ms by calling the Delay(1) function with 1 as a parameter.

3. Otherwise if newSockID is less than 0 this means an error has occurred. Close the main server socket by calling the sl_Close(SockID) function. Print out an error message to the UART.

4. Otherwise, the newSockID contains a valid value. Print out to the UART that the sl_Accept operation succeeded.

14. If the cc3200 has not acquired an ip address then return an error code of –1.

15. Create an integer variable called width and set its value to 320.

16. Create an integer variable called height and set its value to 240.

17. If the camera has not been initialized which means that the g_CameraInit variable is equal to 0 then initialize the camera by calling the InitializeCamera(width, height) function with the width and height parameters created in steps 15 and 16. Set the g_CameraInit variable to 1 to indicate that the camera has just been initialized. This default resolution is called QVGA.

18. While done is less than or equal to 0 do the following:

1. Read data from the TCP socket represented by the newSockID variable that was created in step 13 by calling the sl_Recv(newSockID, uBuf.BsdBuf, BUF_SIZE, 0) function. The first parameter is the socket to read from. The second parameter is the buffer to store the incoming data in. The third parameter is the size of the buffer. The last parameter is not supported in this version of the API. The returned value which is the number of bytes read into the buffer is assigned to the Status variable.

2. If the Status is greater than 0 which means that there is data that was read in then do the following:

    1. Put a terminating character at end of raw data to make it a valid string

    2. Check to see if a "terminate" server command as been sent to the CC3200 from the Android device. If it has then set done to 1 in order exit the loop that reads in the incoming commands from the Android. Print out that a terminate command has been received to the UART.

    3. If the command is not a terminate server command then check to see if the command is a command to take a picture in VGA format. If it is then do the following:

        1. If the current camera resolution is not VGA then change the resolution to VGA by calling the SetCameraResolution(640, 480) function with the width and height parameters for a VGA screen. Set the current camera resolution variable to VGA.

        2. Capture an image from the camera by calling the CameraCaptureImage() function and assigning the return value which is the size of the captured image to the g_ImageSize variable.

        3. Transmit the captured image size to the Android device over wifi by calling the TransmitCapturedImageSize(newSockID) function with the socket handle that was connected to the Android after the sl_Accept() function.

    4. If the command is not the VGA command then check to see if the command in the buffer is the QVGA command. If it is then do the following:

1. If the current camera resolution is not set to QVGA then set the camera resolution to QVGA by calling the SetCameraResolution(320, 240) function with the width and height in pixels of a QVGA image. Set the current camera resolution tracking variable to QVGA.

2. Take a picture with the camera by calling the CameraCaptureImage() function. The size of the image taken is returned which is assigned to the g_ImageSize variable.

3. Send the picture size to the Android device over wifi by calling the TransmitCapturedImageSize(newSockID) function with the socket handle from the sl_Accept() function which represents the wifi connection with the Android device.

5. If the command is not the QVGA command then check to see if the command is the QQVGA command. If it is then do the following:

1. If the current camera resolution is not QQVGA then change the camera resolution by calling the SetCameraResolution(160, 120) with the parameters for the width and height of a QQVGA image. Set the current camera resolution tracking variable to QQVGA.

2. Take a photo with the camera by calling the CameraCaptureImage() function and assign the returned image size to the g_ImageSize variable.

3. Transmit the captured image size to the Android over wifi by calling the TransmitCapturedImageSize(newSockID) function with the socket handle that represents the connection between the Android and CC3200.

6. If the command was not a QQVGA command then check to see if the command was a GetImageData command. If it is then transmit the captured image data to the Android by calling the TransmitCapturedImage(newSockID) function.

3. If the status is less than or equal to 0 then print out an error message to the UART

19. Close the newSockID socket that provided the wifi connection to the Android by calling the sl_Close(newSockID)) function. Print out any errors to the UART that occur.

20. Close the SockID main server socket by calling the sl_Close(SockID) function. Print out any errors to the UART that occur.

21. Return a value of SUCCESS which is 0.

See Listing 4-4.

Listing 4-4. The BsdTcpServer() function

```
static int BsdTcpServer(unsigned short Port)

{

    SlSockAddrIn_t Addr;
```

```
SlSockAddrIn_t LocalAddr;


int idx;

int AddrSize;

int  SockID;

int  Status;

int  newSockID;

long LoopCount = 0;

long  nonBlocking = 1;

int done = -1;


for (idx=0 ; idx<BUF_SIZE ; idx++)

{

   uBuf.BsdBuf[idx] = (char)(idx % 10);

}


LocalAddr.sin_family = SL_AF_INET;

LocalAddr.sin_port = sl_Htons((unsigned short)Port);

LocalAddr.sin_addr.s_addr = 0;


SockID = sl_Socket(SL_AF_INET,SL_SOCK_STREAM, 0);

ASSERT_ON_ERROR(SockID);

if (SockID < 0)

{

        Report("sl_Socket() function FAILED !!!\n\r");

}

else

{

        Report("sl_Socket() operation ok ...\n\r");
```

```
    }


    AddrSize = sizeof(SlSockAddrIn_t);

    Status = sl_Bind(SockID, (SlSockAddr_t *)&LocalAddr, AddrSize);

    if( Status < 0 )

    {

        /* error */

        sl_Close(SockID);

        ASSERT_ON_ERROR(Status);

    }

    else

    {

            Report("sl_Bind operation ok ...\n\r");

    }


    Status = sl_Listen(SockID, 0);

    if( Status < 0 )

    {

        sl_Close(SockID);

        ASSERT_ON_ERROR(Status);

    }

    else

    {

            Report("sl_Listen() operation ok ...\n\r");

    }


    Status = sl_SetSockOpt(SockID, SL_SOL_SOCKET, SL_SO_NONBLOCKING,

                    &nonBlocking, sizeof(nonBlocking));

    ASSERT_ON_ERROR(Status);
```

```
if (Status < 0)

{

        Report("sl_SetSockOpt operation FAILED !!!\n\r");

}

else

{

        Report("sl_SetSockOpt operation ok ... \n\r");

}


Report ("Waiting for sl_Accept operation to complete ... \n\r");

newSockID = SL_EAGAIN;

while( newSockID < 0 &&  IS_IP_ACQUIRED(g_ulStatus))

{

   newSockID = sl_Accept(SockID, ( struct SlSockAddr_t *)&Addr,

                (SlSocklen_t*)&AddrSize);

   if( newSockID == SL_EAGAIN )

   {

      /* Wait for 1 ms */

      Delay(1);

   }

   else if( newSockID < 0 )

   {

      sl_Close(SockID);

      ASSERT_ON_ERROR(newSockID);

      Report ("sl_Accept Error - Socket ID < 0 ...\n\r");

   }

   else

   {

        // Operation Finished
```

```
        Report("sl_Accept operation ok ...\n\r");

    }

}


Report("Finished Accept ...\n\r");

if(! IS_IP_ACQUIRED(g_ulStatus))

{

    return -1;

}


Report ("Ready to recieve data using sl_Recv\n\r");

// Initialize Camera to QVGA resolution

int width = 320;

int height = 240;

if (g_CameraInit == 0)

{

        InitializeCamera(width, height);

        g_CameraInit = 1;

}


while (done <= 0)

{

    Status = sl_Recv(newSockID, uBuf.BsdBuf, BUF_SIZE, 0);

    if (Status > 0)

    {

        // Process incoming data

        // Put terminating character at end of raw data to make it a valid string

        uBuf.BsdBuf[Status] = '\0';
```

```c
// Check if Need to Terminate Server

if (strcmp(uBuf.BsdBuf, "terminate") == 0)

{

        Report("******* Terminate TCP Server Command Issued by Android Client\n\r");

        done = 1;

}

else

if (strcmp(uBuf.BsdBuf, "VGA") == 0)

{

        // Change resolution if needed

        if (g_CameraResolution != VGA)

        {

                // Set VGA Mode

                SetCameraResolution(640, 480);

                g_CameraResolution = VGA;

        }


        // Take Picture and return the size of the image taken

        g_ImageSize = CameraCaptureImage();


        // Send picture size to Android

        TransmitCapturedImageSize(newSockID);

}

else

if (strcmp(uBuf.BsdBuf, "QVGA") == 0)

{

        // Change resolution if needed

        if (g_CameraResolution != QVGA)

        {
```

```
                    // Set QVGA Mode

                    SetCameraResolution(320, 240);

                    g_CameraResolution = QVGA;

            }


                    // Take Picture and return the size of the image taken

                    g_ImageSize = CameraCaptureImage();


                    // Send picture size to Android

                    TransmitCapturedImageSize(newSockID);

        }

        else

if (strcmp(uBuf.BsdBuf, "QQVGA") == 0)

{

        // Change resolution if needed

        if (g_CameraResolution != QQVGA)

        {

                    // Set QVGA Mode

                    SetCameraResolution(160, 120);

                    g_CameraResolution = QQVGA;

        }


        // Take Picture and return the size of the image taken

        g_ImageSize = CameraCaptureImage();


        // Send picture size to Android

        TransmitCapturedImageSize(newSockID);

}

else
```

```
if (strcmp(uBuf.BsdBuf, "GetImageData") == 0)

{

        // Send Image Data for Camera

        TransmitCapturedImage(newSockID);

}

}

else

if( Status <= 0 )

{

    /* error */

    ASSERT_ON_ERROR(sl_Close(newSockID));

    ASSERT_ON_ERROR(sl_Close(SockID));

    ASSERT_ON_ERROR(Status);

    Report("ERROR reading data using sl_Recv() fuction ... \n\r");

}

}


Report ("Finished recieving data ...\n\r");

ASSERT_ON_ERROR(sl_Close(newSockID));

ASSERT_ON_ERROR(sl_Close(SockID));


return SUCCESS;

}
```

Restarting the TCP Server

When the Android sends a "terminate" command when the user exits the application, the TCP server that is running on the CC3200 shuts down and restarts. The TCP server which handles the Android commands and was covered in the previous section is started and restarted in the WlanAPMode() function.

The PORT_NUM is the port number of the TCP server and is defined as 5001.

```
#define PORT_NUM  5001     /* Port to be used  by TCP server*/
```

The portion of the code that starts and restarts the server does the following in an infinite loop:

1. Prints to the UART that the TCP server is starting.

2. Starts the TCP server by calling the BsdTcpServer(PORT_NUM) function with the port number that the server will listen to for incoming connections. When the server is no longer active the return value is assigned to lRetVal.

3. Print out the success or failure status of the server to the UART based on the lRetVal.

4. Go to step 1.

See Listing 4-5.

Listing 4-5. The TCP server loop

```
// TCP Server Loop

// Start TCP Server. If application terminates then terminate current TCP

// Server and start brand new TCP Server and wait for new connection.

while (1)

{

        UART_PRINT("Starting TCP Server ...\n\r");

        lRetVal = BsdTcpServer(PORT_NUM);

        if (lRetVal < 0)

        {

                UART_PRINT("TCP Server Creation Failed !!!\n\r");

        }

        else

        {

                UART_PRINT("TCP Server Creation Succeeded !!!\n\r");

        }

}
```

Summary

In this chapter I gave the reader a basic overview of how the CC3200 wifi worked within the context of this book's home security system. I first covered the basic CC3200 wifi networking modes. Then I covered the key steps that are needed to initialize the CC3200's wifi and put the device into access point mode. I then discussed in detail how the TCP server worked on the CC3200 device including the wifi connection procedure to the Android client device. Finally, I explained how the TCP server is managed when the Android client is disconnected.

Chapter 5

Motion Detection Using a Camera

This chapter covers the motion detection method used in the home security and surveillance system described in this book. I first give the reader an overview of the sum of absolute differences algorithm that is used to detect motion in this book. I follow up by discussing the actual code that implements this algorithm.

Sum of Absolute Differences Motion Detection Method Overview

The definition of the sum of absolute differences is according to Wikipedia:

"In digital image processing, the sum of absolute differences (SAD) is a measure of the similarity between image blocks. It is calculated by taking the absolute difference between each pixel in the original block and the corresponding pixel in the block being used for comparison. These differences are summed to create a simple metric of block similarity, the L1 norm of the difference image or Manhattan distance between two image blocks."

The sum of absolute differences or SAD is the method for motion detection used by the alarm system in this book. The SAD method also captures changes in colors such as that produced by shadows or other changes in lighting.

First a SAD Threshold value needs to be calibrated.

The SAD Threshold value is calibrated by:

1. Calculating the SAD with no movement between two consecutive camera frames. Any differences in the color for pixels between frames are due to variations in the color captured by the camera's image sensor or camera noise.

2. If the SAD value from step one is the highest value so far then set this as the highest SAD value found

3. If the number of iterations for SAD calibration to complete has not yet been reached then go to step 1.

4. Otherwise, calculate the threshold SAD value by adding a value to the highest SAD value calculated from step 1 and 2. The resulting value represents the point where the level in the differences in the two frames will indicate movement.

See Figure 5-1.

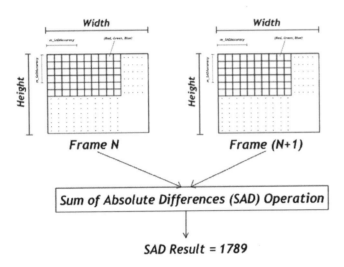

SAD Result = 1789

Figure 5-1. Sum of Absolute Differences Overview

To detect motion, do the following:

1. Calculate the SAD between two consecutive camera frames.

2. If the SAD value is greater than the SAD threshold value then motion has been detected so increment the total number of motions detected.

3. If the total number of motions detected exceeds some target number then trigger the alarm. Otherwise, go back to step 1.

Android Sum of Absolute Differences Calculation Code

The SAD calculation uses two consecutive bitmap images that were captured by the camera and is performed on the Android device. A bitmap image consists of individual units called pixels. A pixel contains color information in the form of red, green, and blue color values. A bitmap also has a width and a height. See Figure 5-2.

The SumAbsoluteDifferenceCalculation() function calculates the SAD for two different bitmaps that are input to the function which are BitmapPrevious which represents the previous bitmap image that was captured from the camera and BitmapCurrent which represents the current bitmap image that was captured.

The SumAbsoluteDifferenceCalculation() function does the following:

1. If the previous bitmap image was null that means that this is the first image to be processed for SAD and thus the SAD result is 0 for no differences between images.

2. Calculate the height of the previous frame by calling the BitmapPrevious.getHeight() function and assigning the result to HeightPrev.

3. Calculate the width of the previous bitmap by calling the BitmapPrevious.getWidth() function and assigning the return value to WidthPrev.

4. Calculate the height of the current bitmap by calling the BitmapCurrent.getHeight() function and assigning the return value to HeightCur.

5. Calculate the width of the current bitmap by calling the BitmapCurrent.getWidth() function and assigning the return value to WidthCur.

6. Check if this is the first bitmap processed or if there is a change in resolution. If either case is true either HeightPrev will be different from HeightCur or WidthPrev will be different from WidthCur. The SAD value in this case is 0.

7. For each pixel along the height of the current resolution of bitmap with m_SADAccuracy spacing and for each pixel along the width of the current resolution of bitmap with m_SADAccuracy spacing do the following:

    1. Get the color for a Pixel on the previous bitmap by calling the BitmapPrevious.getPixel(x,y) function and storing the result in the ColorPrev variable. The x input parameter is the horizontal position of the pixel and the y input parameter is the vertical position of the pixel.

    2. Get the red component of the color retrieved in step 1 by calling the Color.red(ColorPrev) function and assigning the returned value to RedPrev.

    3. Get the green component of the color retrieved in step 1 by calling the Color.green(ColorPrev) function and assigning the returned value to GreenPrev.

    4. Get the blue component of the color retrieved in step 1 by calling the Color.blue(ColorPrev) function and assigning the returned value to BluePrev.

    5. Get the color for the pixel on the current bitmap by calling the BitmapCurrent.getPixel(x,y) function and storing the result in the ColorCur variable. The x input parameter is the horizontal position of the pixel and the y input parameter is the vertical position of the pixel.

    6. Get the red component of the color retrieved in step 5 by calling the Color.red(ColorCur) function and assigning the result to the RedCur variable.

    7. Get the green component of the color retrieved in step 5 by calling the Color.green(ColorCur) function and assigning the result to the GreenCur variable.

    8. Get the blue color component of the color retrieved in step 5 by calling the Color.blue(ColorCur) function and assigning the result to the BlueCur variable.

    9. Calculate the absolute difference between the red components of the pixel in the current bitmap and the corresponding pixel in the previous bitmap by calling the Math.abs(RedCur -RedPrev) function. The input parameter is the difference between the red components of the color. This result is stored in the RedDiff variable.

    10. Calculate the absolute difference between the green components of the pixel in the current bitmap and the corresponding pixel in the previous bitmap by calling the

Math.abs(GreenCur - GreenPrev) function. The input parameter is the difference between the green color components in the current and previous bitmaps. The result is stored in the GreenDiff variable.

11. Calculate the absolute difference between the blue components of the pixel in the current bitmap and the corresponding pixel in the previous bitmap by calling the Math.abs(BlueCur - BluePrev) function. The input parameter is the difference between the blue color components of the current and previous bitmaps. The result is stored in the BlueDiff variable.

12. Compute the average of the color differences between the 3 color channels red, green, and blue for a pixel by adding the RedDiff, BlueDiff, and GreenDiff variables and dividing the sum by 3. The result is then stored in the ColorDiffAverage variable.

13. Add this average difference for this pixel to the running total for the color differences for all the pixels in the image by adding the ColorDiffAverage to SAD

8. Return the final value of SAD that is the sum of all the absolute differences of all the pixels in the image.

See Listing 5-1. A close up of a bitmap image is shown in Figure 5-2.

Listing 5-1. The SumAbsoluteDifferenceCalculation() function

```
int SumAbsoluteDifferenceCalculation(Bitmap BitmapPrevious, Bitmap BitmapCurrent)

{

        int SAD = 0;

        int HeightPrev = 0;

        int WidthPrev = 0;


        int HeightCur  = 0;

        int WidthCur  = 0;


        if (BitmapPrevious == null)

        {

                return 0;

        }


        // Calculate dimensions of previous frame
```

```
HeightPrev = BitmapPrevious.getHeight();

WidthPrev = BitmapPrevious.getWidth();


// Calculate dimensions of current frame

HeightCur = BitmapCurrent.getHeight();

WidthCur = BitmapCurrent.getWidth();


// Check if this is first bitmap processed.

if ((HeightPrev != HeightCur) ||

(WidthPrev  != WidthCur))

{

        // Since previous image is

        // of a different dimension then the SADD will be 0

        return 0;

}


// Calculate the SAD for the two input Bitmaps

for (int y=0; y<HeightCur; y=y+m_SADAccuracy)

{

        for (int x=0; x<WidthCur; x=x+m_SADAccuracy)

        {

                // Get Color for Pixel on Previous Bitmap

                int ColorPrev      =        BitmapPrevious.getPixel(x,y);

                int RedPrev        =        Color.red(ColorPrev);

                int GreenPrev      =        Color.green(ColorPrev);

                int BluePrev       =        Color.blue(ColorPrev);


                // Get Color for Pixel on Current Bitmap

                int ColorCur       =        BitmapCurrent.getPixel(x,y);
```

```
        int RedCur          =          Color.red(ColorCur);

        int GreenCur        =          Color.green(ColorCur);

        int BlueCur         =          Color.blue(ColorCur);


        // Calculate the absolute difference between the Pixels

        int RedDiff         =          Math.abs(RedCur  - RedPrev);

        int GreenDiff       =          Math.abs(GreenCur -  GreenPrev);

        int BlueDiff        =          Math.abs(BlueCur  - BluePrev);


        // Take the average of the color differences between the 3 color channels

        int ColorDiffAverage = (RedDiff + BlueDiff + GreenDiff)/3;


        // Add this average difference to the running total for SAD

        SAD = SAD + ColorDiffAverage;

            }
        }


        return SAD;

    }
```

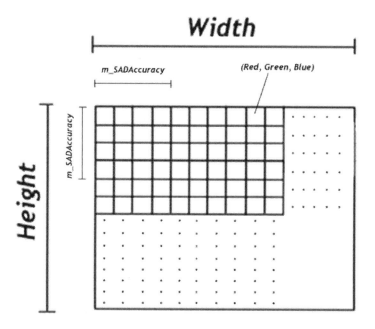

Figure 5-2. A close up of a bitmap frame

Summary

In this chapter I covered the method that is used to detect motion by the camera in this home security and surveillance system. I first gave a general overview of the sum of absolute differences method that I used for motion detection. I then gave an in depth presentation of the Android source code that is used to implement the sum of absolute differences or SAD motion detection algorithm.

Chapter 6

The Android Wireless Security System Design

In this chapter I cover the security system design for the Android side of the home security and surveillance system described in this book. I start off with an overview of the security system design and how the Android and the CC3200 devices interact with one another. Next, I cover how sound effects are implemented on the Android side of the system. Finally, I discuss how the main alarm system logic, motion detection, user interface, and cell phone communication systems are implemented inside the MainActivity class.

GotchaCAM Security System Overview

The security system presented in this book is called the "GotchaCAM" and consists of two parts which are the Android device portion and the CC3200 device portion. The CC3200 portion consists of the CC3200 Simplelink device that is in my case the ArduCAM CC3200 Uno board. The MT9D111 camera takes the actual photos and is attached to the camera port on the CC3200 board. The Android portion of the security system consists of an Android cell phone that handles motion detection, alarm logic, user interface, and cell phone communication. The connection between the two portions is through a wifi connection. The CC3200 device is put into access point mode which provides for its own self contained network. The Android device connects to this access point and communicates with the CC3200 device.

The general operation of the GotchaCAM security system is that:

1. The Android device is running a client that initiates a wifi connection with the CC3200 device.

2. The CC3200 device runs a TCP server which listens to a specific port for a connection request. If one is requested then a wifi connection is established.

3. The Android device sends a command using wifi to the CC3200 device.

4. The CC3200 processes this command and sends the requested data to the Android device.

5. Steps 3 and 4 are repeated until a "terminate" command is sent from the Android device to the CC3200.

6. The CC3200 exits the current TCP server connection and then restarts a new TCP server.

An important thing to note is that the CC3200 device just takes the picture, stores the picture on the CC3200 onboard memory, and then sends the data using wifi to the Android device. All the other features such as motion detection are done on the Android device.

See Figure 6-1.

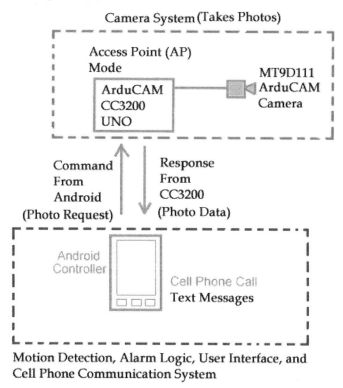

Figure 6-1. Overview of the GotchaCAM Security System

Android Sound Effects

This section discusses the sound effects in the Android program. I first discuss the class that is used for the sound effects which is the Sound class. I then show how this class is used in the MainActivity class to initialize the sounds for the Android program.

The Custom Sound Class

The Sound class is a custom class that is responsible for playing back digital sounds.

The m_SoundPool variable holds a SoundPool class object that was created in the MainActivity class. The SoundPool object is the main interface to loading in, playing back, and managing our sounds.

```
private SoundPool m_SoundPool;
```

The m_SoundIndex variable holds the identification number of the sound. The number is the ID of the sound within m_SoundPool.

```
private int m_SoundIndex = -1;
```

The m_LeftVolume variable holds a value from 0 no volume to 1 full volume of the left channel of a stereo sound.

float m_LeftVolume = 1;

The m_RightVolume variable holds a value from 0 no volume to 1 full volume of the right channel of a stereo sound.

float m_RightVolume = 1;

The m_Priority variable holds the streaming priority of the sound with 0 being the lowest priority.

int m_Priority = 1;

If the m_Loop variable is set to –1 then the sound is set to loop continuously. If it is 0 then the sound is set to play one time.

int m_Loop = 0;

The m_Rate variable is the speed that the sound is played back. A 1 setting is normal playback speed. The range is from 0.5 to 2.0. The variable is initialized to 1.

float m_Rate = 1;

The m_StreamID variable holds the identification number of the sound stream that is currently playing the actual sound.

int m_StreamID = 0;

The Sound class constructor creates a Sound class object by loading in and initializing the sound designated by the ResourceID input parameter and putting it inside the existing SoundPool class object designated by the Pool input parameter. The Activity class object also must be input as the iContext parameter.

More specifically:

1. The global class variable m_SoundPool is set to the Pool input parameter.

2. The sound is loaded into the m_SoundPool class object by calling the m_SoundPool.load(iContext, ResourceID, 1) function. This function also returns the index number for the newly created sound in the SoundPool object. This index is then assigned to m_SoundIndex.

See Listing 6-1.

Listing 6-1. The Sound constructor

```
Sound(Context iContext, SoundPool Pool, int ResourceID)

{

        m_SoundPool = Pool;
```

```
m_SoundIndex = m_SoundPool.load(iContext, ResourceID, 1);
```

}

The PlaySound() function plays the sound through the Android device's speakers. PlaySound(true) plays the sound in a continuous infinite loop. A PlaySound(false) plays the sound one time only.

More specifically the function does the following:

1. If the m_Loop variable is equal to –1 then this sound is set to continuously play so there is no need to play it again so return without doing anything further.

2. If the input parameter Loop is set to true then set m_Loop to –1 to indicate this sound needs to be looped continuously. Otherwise, set m_Loop to 0.

3. Start playing the sound effect by calling the m_SoundPool.play(m_SoundIndex, m_LeftVolume, m_RightVolume, m_Priority, m_Loop, m_Rate) function. The m_SoundIndex parameter indicates the sound within the sound pool that should be played back. The m_LeftVolume and m_RightVolume indicate the volume levels of the sound's left and right channels. The next parameters indicate the priority, whether to loop the sound or not, and the speed at which to play the sound back. The id number of the stream that is playing back the sound is returned by the function and stored in the m_StreamID class variable.

See Listing 6-2.

Listing 6-2. The PlaySound() function

```
void PlaySound(boolean Loop)

{

        //public final int play (int soundID, float leftVolume, float rightVolume, int priority, int loop, float rate)

        // Sound already playing

        if (m_Loop == -1)

        {

                return;

        }

        if (Loop)

        {

                m_Loop = -1;

        }

        else
```

```
        {
                m_Loop = 0;
        }

        m_StreamID = m_SoundPool.play(m_SoundIndex, m_LeftVolume, m_RightVolume, m_Priority, m_Loop,
m_Rate);
}
```

The StopSound() function stops the sound playing by:

1. Calling the m_SoundPool.stop(m_StreamID) function with the id number of the stream associated with this playing sound.

2. Setting the m_Loop variable to 0 to indicate that this sound is not to be looped.

See Listing 6-3.

Listing 6-3. The StopSound() function

```
void StopSound()
{
        m_SoundPool.stop(m_StreamID);

        m_Loop = 0;
}
```

The GetSoundPool() function returns m_SoundPool which is a reference to the sound pool that is being used by this Sound class object. See Listing 6-4.

Listing 6-4. The GetSoundPool() function

```
SoundPool GetSoundPool()
{
        return m_SoundPool;
}
```

Initializing and Using the Sound Class

The Sound class is used in the MainActivity class for such things like playing sounds for indicating an intruder has been detected.

The SoundPool class needs to be imported using the import keyword

import android.media.SoundPool;

The m_SoundPool variable is declared as a SoundPool class object and is initialized to null.

private SoundPool m_SoundPool = null;

Two variables that are references to the Sound class are declared and initialized to null. These variables are m_Alert1SFX and m_Alert2SFX.

private Sound m_Alert1SFX = null;

private Sound m_Alert2SFX = null;

The CreateSound() function creates new Sound class objects for use with our intruder alarm system.

The function does the following:

1. Creates a new Sound object using the .wav sound file located in the res\raw folder of the main workspace directory for this project. This is done by calling the Sound constructor with the resource id for this sound file which is R.raw.playershoot2. This sound effect is played when the "Take Photo" button is pressed.

2. Creates a new Sound object using the .wav sound file located in the res\raw folder of the main workspace directory for this project. This is done by calling the Sound constructor with the resource id for this sound file which is R.raw.explosion1. This sound effect is played when an intruder has been detected or a photo has finished loading in for the home security system.

Note: The R class is a globally available built in and automatically generated class that contains resource ids that link to the actual sound files which are wave files located in the res\raw directory of the Android project. You can record your own wave files, copy the files into this directory and change these lines of code to change the sounds being played for functions.

See Listing 6-5.

Listing 6-5. The CreateSound() function

```
void CreateSound(Context iContext)

{

        m_Alert1SFX = new Sound(iContext, m_SoundPool, R.raw.playershoot2);

        m_Alert2SFX = new Sound(iContext, m_SoundPool, R.raw.explosion1);

}
```

The StopSounds() function stops all the sound effects from playing by calling the StopSound() function on each of the Sound class objects. See Listing 6-6.

Listing 6-6. The StopSounds() function

```
void StopSounds()

{

        m_Alert1SFX.StopSound();

        m_Alert2SFX.StopSound();

}
```

The CreateSoundPool() function creates a new SoundPool object by:

1. Calling the SoundPool constructor SoundPool(maxStreams, streamType, srcQuality) with the following input parameters:

    1. maxStreams - The maximum number of simultaneous streams for this SoundPool object. A value of 10 is assigned

    2. streamType - The audio stream type as described in AudioManager. This is set to a value of STREAM_MUSIC.

    3. srcQuality - the sample-rate converter quality. Currently has no effect. Set to 0 for the default setting

2. The newly created SoundPool class object is then assigned to m_SoundPool.

See Listing 6-7.

Listing 6-7. The CreateSoundPool() function

```
void CreateSoundPool()

{

        int maxStreams = 10;

        int streamType = AudioManager.STREAM_MUSIC;

        int srcQuality = 0;


        m_SoundPool = new SoundPool(maxStreams, streamType, srcQuality);

        if (m_SoundPool == null)

        {
```

```
Log.e("Main Activity " , "m_SoundPool creation failure!!!!!!!!!!!!!!!!!!!!!!!!!!!!!!!!!!!!!!!!!!!!!!!!!!!!!!");

        }

    }
```

The MainActivity Class

The MainActivity class contains the main code for the alarm. The code to handle motion detection, the user interface, the alarm system logic, and the cell phone communication system are all contained in this class. The rest of this chapter covers the functions and other code relating to the MainActivity Class.

The MainActivity class extends the Activity class and implements the Runnable interface by implementing the run() function. The class is declared as:

public class MainActivity extends Activity implements Runnable

The key functions in this class are:

- onCreate() – This function is called when the Android application is created and is used to initialize the security system.

- OnOptionsItemSelected() – This function is called when the user touches items in the graphical user interface belonging to the application.

- run() – This function is called from another thread and is used to process incoming data and to update the graphical user interface after new information is loaded into the Android from the CC3200.

- onDestroy() – This function is called when the application ends and is used to shut down the wifi connection and other items.

The MainActivity Class Variables

The TAG String object variable is used with the Log() function for debugging purposes to indicate that an error or debug message came from the MainActivity class.

String TAG = "GotchaCAM";

The version of this application is held in the m_Version String variable.

String m_Version = "GotchaCAM Version 1.0 \n";

The copyright notice for this application is held in m_Copyright and is a text string.

String m_Copyright = "Copyright 2016 Robert Chin. All rights reserved.\n";

The m_EmergencyPhoneNumber variable holds the phone number for the Android to call if there is an intruder detected by the alarm system. This number is set by the user in the phone entry text box on the Android application.

String m_EmergencyPhoneNumber ="";

The m_EmergencyPhoneNumberHandle variable holds the shared preferences handle that is used to save and then load in the value of the emergency phone number.

String m_EmergencyPhoneNumberHandle = "PhoneNumber";

The m_GotchaCamPreferencesFile holds all the saved preference handles and the associated data for the security application including the handle and data pair for the emergency phone number.

String m_GotchaCamPreferencesFile = "GotchaCamRecords";

If m_CallOutDone is true then the required emergency callout has already been completed. Otherwise the value is false.

boolean m_CallOutDone = false;

The m_EmergencyMessageRepeatTimes variable holds the number of times to repeat the vocal alarm generated by Android's text to speech function. For example, the default number of times to repeat the phrase "Intruder Alert Intruder has been detected by the motion sensor" is set to 5 times.

int m_EmergencyMessageRepeatTimes = 5;

The m_EmergencyMessageDone variable is true if the required speech warning of an intruder alert has started to execute and false otherwise.

boolean m_EmergencyMessageDone = false;

The m_NumberMotionsDetected variable holds the number of motions detected by the SAD (Sum of Absolute Differences) algorithm.

int m_NumberMotionsDetected = 0;

The m_ServerStaticIP variable holds the ip address of the CC3200 server.

String m_ServerStaticIP = "10.1.1.1";

The TextMessageSetting enumeration contains the possible values of the emergency text message alert setting. The TEXT_OFF value means that no emergency text messages will be sent. The TEXT_ON value means that emergency text messages will be sent

enum TextMessageSetting

{

      TEXT_OFF,

      TEXT_ON

};

The m_AlarmSet value is true if the security system is on. The value is false otherwise.

boolean m_AlarmSet = false;

The m_AlarmTripped variable is true if the alarm has been activated by the detection of an intruder. It is false otherwise.

```
boolean m_AlarmTripped = false;
```

The m_CallOutSet variable is true if the alarm system is set to call out to the emergency phone number when an intruder is detected. If it is false then the an intruder alert message just appears locally on the debug window of the Android application and a sound is played continuously and a text speech voice is played to announce that an intruder has been detected by the motion detector.

```
boolean m_CallOutSet = true;
```

The m_TextMessagesSetting holds the current status of the emergency text message alert setting. This value is defaulted to TEXT_ON which sends out an emergency text message to the emergency phone number when an intruder is detected.

```
TextMessageSetting m_TextMessagesSetting = TextMessageSetting.TEXT_ON;
```

The m_TextMessageSent variable is true if an emergency text message has been sent after the alarm has been tripped and false otherwise.

```
boolean m_TextMessageSent = false;
```

The m_TTS variable is used for text to speech conversion so that the Android device can vocalize such things as intruder alerts and important system messages.

```
TextToSpeech m_TTS = null;
```

The m_PortNumber variable is the port that the TCP server running on the CC3200 is listening to for a connection request.

```
int m_PortNumber = 5001;
```

The m_WifiMessageHandler variable processes the data being returned from the CC3200.

```
WifiMessageHandler m_WifiMessageHandler = null;
```

The m_ClientConnectThread is the class object that will be used to establish a wifi connection with the CC3200 as well as send commands to the CC3200.

```
Client m_ClientConnectThread = null;
```

The m_TakePhotoButtonActive variable is true if the "Take Photo" button is active and able to be pressed. If it is false then the button is not active and can not be pressed.

```
boolean  m_TakePhotoButtonActive=false;
```

The m_TakePhotoButton represents the "Take Photo" button which the user presses to take a photo with the camera attached to the CC3200 device and have it sent back to the Android for display.

```
Button    m_TakePhotoButton= null;
```

The Resolution enumeration defines the camera image capture resolutions available which are QQVGA which is 160 by 120 pixels, QVGA 320 by 240 pixels, and VGA which is 640 by 480 pixels.

```
enum Resolution

{

        QQVGA,

        QVGA,

        VGA

};
```

The m_Resolution variable is the image resolution for the photo that was captured by the CC3200 and is currently being transmitted to the Android for display.

```
Resolution m_Resolution = Resolution.QVGA;
```

The m_PhotoSize variable holds the size of the image in bytes that was taken by the MT9D111 camera.

```
int m_PhotoSize = 0;
```

The m_PhotoData variable points to the received binary photo image data.

```
byte[] m_PhotoData= null;
```

The m_InfoTextView TextView class object holds image resolution information and other security system settings.

```
TextView m_InfoTextView   = null;
```

The m_TakePhotoCallbackDone variable is true if a command related to a "Take Photo" button press has just completed and is in need of processing. It is false otherwise.

```
boolean m_TakePhotoCallbackDone = false;
```

The TakePhotoCallbackState enumeration describes the two stages of taking a photo. The first stage is getting the size of the captured image from the CC3200 and the second stage is getting the actual image data from the CC3200 using the image size to determine when all the binary data has been transmitted.

```
enum TakePhotoCallbackState

{

        GetImageSize,

        GetImageData

};
```

The m_TakePhotoState variable holds the current stage that the "Take Photo" command is in

TakePhotoCallbackState m_TakePhotoState;

The m_SurveillanceActive variable is true if camera surveillance is active and photos are continuously taken by the MT9D111 camera and sent to the Android.

boolean   m_SurveillanceActive = false;

The m_SurveillanceFrameNumber variable holds the current number of the surveillance photo taken.

int m_SurveillanceFrameNumber = 0;

The m_SurveillanceFileName is the file name that a photo is saved under if Android storage is turned on.

String   m_SurveillanceFileName = "";

The AndroidStorage enumeration is StoreYes if storing received images is turned on. If the value is StoreNo then received images from the CC3200 are not stored on the Android's file system. If the system is in "Surveilance" mode then after the alarm is tripped then any image frames with detected motions will be stored if StoreYes is selected. Otherwise, no images will be stored while in "Surveillance" mode.

enum AndroidStorage

{

        StoreYes,

        StoreNo

}

The m_AndroidStorage variable determines if incoming pictures from the CC3200 are stored on the Android's file system. The default value is that pictures are not stored.

AndroidStorage m_AndroidStorage = AndroidStorage.StoreNo;

The m_AndroidPicsDirectory variable holds the name of the directory to save pictures under.

String m_AndroidPicsDirectory = "CAMPics";

The m_CameraDir holds the Android picture directory designated by the Android operating system.

File m_CameraDir;

The m_PhoneEntryView is a text entry box that allows the user to enter the emergency phone number.

EditText m_PhoneEntryView = null;

The m_DebugMsgView represents the Debug Window on the Android app that displays the debug information for the application as well as intruder alerts.

EditText m_DebugMsgView =null;

The m_DebugMsg string holds the text that will be displayed in the Debug Message Window.

String m_DebugMsg= "";

If m_RefreshMessageWindows is true then the m_DebugMsg string is printed to the debug message window.

boolean m_RefreshMessageWindows = false;

This is not used in the current alarm system but provides an example of how to read in text data in general from the CC3200 and have the returned information displayed in the debug message window. If this value is true then display the incoming text data from the CC3200.

boolean m_RecieveTextDataCallBackDone = false;

The m_MaxFileNames variable holds the maximum number of image file names that can be loaded from the m_AndroidPicsDirectory and selected by the user to view.

int m_MaxFileNames = 500;

The m_NumberFileNames variable holds the number of files contained in the m_AndroidPicsDirectory.

int m_NumberFileNames = 0;

The m_AndroidFileGroupID and m_AndroidFileItemID variables help identify which files are located on the Android file system.

int m_AndroidFileGroupID = 95;

int m_AndroidFileItemID = 35;

The m_AndroidFileNames string array holds a complete list of the names of the files located in the Android's picture directory

String[] m_AndroidFileNames = new String[m_MaxFileNames];

The m_SAD variable holds the sum of absolute difference between two consecutive image frames captured from the MT9D111 camera attached to the CC3200.

int m_SAD = 0;

The m_SADAccuracy variable determines the spacing of the pixels in the image that are used for the SAD (Sum of Absolute Differences) calculation. For example, a value of 8 would mean that every 8th pixel in the horizontal and vertical direction would be used to calculate the SAD value.

int m_SADAccuracy = 8;

If the calculated value of the SAD from two consecutive frames is greater than the value of m_SADThreshold then there has been movement.

int m_SADThreshold = 0;

The m_SADCount variable holds the number of times the SAD value has been calculated for the initial calibration before activating the security system's motion detection.

```
int m_SADCount = 0;
```

The m_SADCalcNumIterations variable holds the number of times to calculate the SAD value for the initial SAD calibration when the motion detection alarm is activated.

```
int m_SADCalcNumIterations = 10; // Number of iterations for SAD Threshold calculation
```

The m_SADHighest variable holds the largest value of SAD calculated for the motion detection calibration.

```
int m_SADHighest = 0;
```

The m_SADCalcThreshold variable holds the calculated value of the SAD threshold based on the highest value of SAD from the SAD calibration added to a percentage of the highest SAD value.

```
int m_SADCalcThreshold = 0;
```

The m_SADTripped value is a value that is greater than the m_SADThreshold value and indicates the exact SAD value that tripped the motion detection alarm.

```
int m_SADTripped = 0;
```

The m_SADThresholdPercentError variable is used in the calculation of the SAD threshold value.

```
double m_SADThresholdPercentError = 0.10;
```

The m_SADCalibrationDone variable is true if the SAD calibration has finished and the SAD threshold value has been determined.

```
boolean m_SADCalibrationDone = false;
```

The m_BitmapPrevious variable holds the previous image frame that was transmitted to the Android device from the CC3200.

```
Bitmap m_BitmapPrevious=null;
```

The m_BitmapCurrent variable holds the current image frame that was transmitted to the Android device from the CC3200.

```
Bitmap m_BitmapCurrent=null;
```

The m_CurTime variable holds the current Android system time in milliseconds

```
long m_CurTime = 0;
```

The m_MinimumMotionsForAlarmTrip variable holds the minimum number of detected motions that need to occur for alarm to be tripped.

```
int m_MinimumMotionsForAlarmTrip = 5;
```

In order for the alarm to trip the minimum number of motions need to be detected within a certain amount of time which is held in the m_FalsePositiveTimeInterval variable in milliseconds. This is called the false positive alarm trip test.

```
long m_FalsePositiveTimeInterval = 1000 * 10;
```

The m_FalsePositiveTestStarted value is false if the test for screening out false positive alarms has not started yet.

boolean m_FalsePositiveTestStarted = false;

The m_FalsePositiveStartTime variable holds the system time in milliseconds that the false positive test for the tripping of the intruder alarm has started.

long m_FalsePositiveStartTime = 0;

The onCreate() Function

The onCreate() function in the MainActivity class is executed when the application is created and contains the code for the initialization of the security system. The @Override keyword before the function indicates that this function overrides the same function in a parent class.

The onCreate() function does the following:

1. Calls the parent function by calling the super.onCreate(savedInstanceState) function with the input parameter to the function savedInstanceState.

2. Sets the Android user interface layout by calling the setContentView(R.layout.activity_main) function with the resource id for the main activity layout as the input parameter.

3. Fixes the screen orientation of the Android screen to the portrait orientation by calling the this.setRequestedOrientation(ActivityInfo.SCREEN_ORIENTATION_PORTRAIT) function. The screen orientation is maintained regardless of the orientation of the Android device during the execution of the application.

4. The computerized voice that is used to read out plain text for alerts and information is initialized by calling the TextToSpeechInit() function.

5. Initializes the sound pool that manages the playback and loading of the sound effects by calling the CreateSoundPool() function.

6. Initializes the application's sound effects by calling the CreateSound(this) function.

7. Finds the phone entry text edit box from the Android user interface by calling the (EditText) findViewById(R.id.phoneentry) function with the resource id number for the phone entry text box. Assign the returned value to m_PhoneEntryView.

8. Sets the phone entry text edit box to focusable by calling the m_PhoneEntryView.setFocusable(true) function with the true parameter. If an edit text box is focusable that means the user can click on it and then enter text into it using the Android keyboard.

9. Sets a function to execute when the phone entry edit text box is clicked by the user by calling the m_PhoneEntryView.setOnClickListener() function with a newly created View.OnClickListener() object which stops the notification sound effect from being played. This is done by calling the m_Alert2SFX.StopSound() function.

10. Loads in the emergency call out phone number that is stored on the Android's internal storage system by calling the LoadInPhoneNumber() function.

11. Sets the emergency phone number read in from step 10 into the phone text edit box by calling the m_PhoneEntryView.setText(m_EmergencyPhoneNumber) function with the phone number as a parameter.

12. Find the debug message edit text window by calling the (EditText) findViewById(R.id.debugmsg) function with the resource id of the debug message window and assign the return value to m_DebugMsgView.

13. Adds the application version number to the m_DebugMsg String object.

14. Adds the copyright message to the m_DebugMsg String object.

15. Adds the emergency phone number to the m_DebugMsg String object.

16. Sets the debug message window with the contents of the m_DebugMsg String object by calling the m_DebugMsgView.setText(m_DebugMsg.toCharArray(), 0, m_DebugMsg.length()) function.

17. Disable the debug message window's ability to get the focus by calling the m_DebugMsgView.setFocusable(false) function with the false parameter. This means that the window can not receive text input from the user though touching the window and entering the text using the Android keyboard.

18. Set a new OnClickListener function for the m_DebugMsgView window that stops any notification sounds being played by calling the m_Alert2SFX.StopSound() function.

19. Sets a new OnEditorActionListener object for the phone entry edit text box by calling the m_PhoneEntryView.setOnEditorActionListener() function. The function does the following if the "done" key has been pressed:

    1. Sets the m_EmergencyPhoneNumber to the value the user entered in the phone entry edit text box.

    2. Next, it displays a short message called a toast by calling the Toast() function notifying the user that the emergency phone number has been changed.

    3. Next, it erases the current message being displayed in the debug window and adds a message that notifies the user that the emergency phone number has changed.

    4. Next, it hides the Android keyboard from the user by calling the HideKeyboard() function.

    5. Finally, it saves the phone number to the Android device's permanent storage by calling the SavePhoneNumber() function.

20. Finds the settings information text box by calling the (TextView) findViewById(R.id.textView1) function with the resource id for the information text box. The returned value is assigned to m_InfoTextView.

21. Updates the settings information text box by calling the UpdateCommandTextView() function.

22. The settings information text box is disabled for editing by calling the m_InfoTextView.setFocusable(false) function with false as a parameter.

23. Initialize the Android file storage by calling the InitExternalStorage() function.

24. Finds the take photo button from the Android's layout by calling the (Button) findViewById(R.id.TestMessageButton) function with the resource id of the take photo button as the input parameter. Assigns the result to m_TakePhotoButton.

25. Enables the take photo button so the button can be activated by the user touching it by calling the m_TakePhotoButton.setEnabled(true) function with the true parameter.

26. Create a new OnClickListener() object for the take photo button by calling the m_TakePhotoButton.setOnClickListener() function. The onClick() function that is created sends a camera command that tells the CC3200 device to take a photo. The onClick() function does the following when the user presses the "take photo" button:

    1. Plays a sound effect by calling the m_Alert1SFX.PlaySound(false) function with false as a parameter to indicate that this sound will not loop but be played only once.

    2. Converts the current target image capture resolution to a string by calling the m_Resolution.toString() function and storing the result in the Command variable.

    3. Clears the wifi message handler of old stored data and prepares it to accept new data by calling the m_WifiMessageHandler.ResetData() function.

    4. Sets the command type that will be used to process the incoming data from the CC3200 by calling the m_WifiMessageHandler.SetCommand("GetImageSize") function with the "GetImageSize" parameter which is the command type.

    5. Set the m_TakePhotoState variable to TakePhotoCallbackState.GetImageSize to indicate that the Android is waiting on the CC3200 to send the size of the image that it has just captured.

    6. If the client thread is connected which means that m_ClientConnectThread.IsConnected() evaluates to true then disable the take photo button and send the command to the CC3200 over wifi by calling the m_ClientConnectThread.write(Command.getBytes()) function. The function's parameter converts the Command String object into an array of bytes before sending it over wifi to the CC3200.

27. Create the client socket connection thread and begin its execution that is designed to connect the Android to the CC3200 using wifi by calling the CreateClientConnection(m_ServerStaticIP, m_PortNumber) function. The first parameter is the ip address of the CC3200 device and the second parameter is the port number that the TCP server on the CC3200 is listening to for a connection request.

28. Sets the m_PhotoData array to point to the incoming image data by calling the m_WifiMessageHandler.GetBinaryData() function.

See Listing 6-8.

Listing 6-8. The onCreate() function

```
@Override

protected void onCreate(Bundle savedInstanceState) {

        super.onCreate(savedInstanceState);
```

```
setContentView(R.layout.activity_main);


// Set Orientation for Portrait

this.setRequestedOrientation(ActivityInfo.SCREEN_ORIENTATION_PORTRAIT);


// Initialize Text to Speech engine

TextToSpeechInit();


// Init Sounds

CreateSoundPool();

CreateSound(this);


// Initialize the Output Message Window

m_PhoneEntryView = (EditText) findViewById(R.id.phoneentry);

m_PhoneEntryView.setFocusable(true);

m_PhoneEntryView.setOnClickListener(new View.OnClickListener()

{

        public void onClick(View v)

        {

                m_Alert2SFX.StopSound();

        }

});


LoadInPhoneNumber();

m_PhoneEntryView.setText(m_EmergencyPhoneNumber);


// Initialize the Debug Message Window

m_DebugMsgView = (EditText) findViewById(R.id.debugmsg);

m_DebugMsg = m_Version + "\n";
```

```
m_DebugMsg += m_Copyright + "\n";

m_DebugMsg += "Emergency Phone Number: " + m_EmergencyPhoneNumber + "\n\n";

m_DebugMsgView.setText(m_DebugMsg.toCharArray(), 0, m_DebugMsg.length());

m_DebugMsgView.setFocusable(false);

m_DebugMsgView.setOnClickListener(new View.OnClickListener()

{

        public void onClick(View v)

        {

                m_Alert2SFX.StopSound();

        }

});


m_PhoneEntryView.setOnEditorActionListener(new TextView.OnEditorActionListener() {
    @Override
    public boolean onEditorAction(TextView view, int actionId, KeyEvent event) {
        int result = actionId & EditorInfo.IME_MASK_ACTION;
        switch(result) {
            case EditorInfo.IME_ACTION_DONE:
                // done stuff
                m_EmergencyPhoneNumber = m_PhoneEntryView.getText().toString();
                Log.e(TAG,"In setOnEditorActionListener:: Emergency PhoneNumber = " +
m_EmergencyPhoneNumber);
                Toast.makeText(MainActivity.this, "Emergency Phone Number Changed to " +
m_EmergencyPhoneNumber, Toast.LENGTH_LONG).show();
                m_DebugMsg = "";
                AddDebugMessage("Emergency Phone Number Changed to " +
m_EmergencyPhoneNumber);
                HideKeyboard();
                SavePhoneNumber();
                break;
        }
```

```
                    return true;

                }

});


// Initialize the Information Text window

m_InfoTextView = (TextView) findViewById(R.id.textView1);

UpdateCommandTextView();

m_InfoTextView.setFocusable(false);


// Init External Storage

InitExternalStorage();


// Initialize Test Message Button

m_TakePhotoButton = (Button) findViewById(R.id.TestMessageButton);

m_TakePhotoButton.setEnabled(true);

m_TakePhotoButton.setOnClickListener(new View.OnClickListener()

{

        public void onClick(View v)

        {

                // Perform action on click

                m_Alert1SFX.PlaySound(false);


                // Send Take Photo Command to CC3200

                String Command = m_Resolution.toString();


                // Set Up Data Handler

                m_WifiMessageHandler.ResetData();

                m_WifiMessageHandler.SetCommand("GetImageSize");

                m_TakePhotoState = TakePhotoCallbackState.GetImageSize;
```

```
                    if (m_ClientConnectThread != null)

                    {

                            if (m_ClientConnectThread.IsConnected())

                            {

                                    m_TakePhotoButtonActive = false;

                                    m_TakePhotoButton.setEnabled(false);


                                    m_ClientConnectThread.write(Command.getBytes());

                                    m_DebugMsg += "Sending 'Take Photo' Command! COMMAND =
" + Command + "\n";

                            }

                            else

                            {

                                    m_DebugMsg += "ERROR! ClientConnectedThread is not
connected!! \n";

                                    Log.e(TAG,"ERROR! ClientConnectedThread is not connected!!");

                                    if (m_TTS != null)

                                    {

                                            m_TTS.speak("ERROR ClientConnectedThread is not
connected", TextToSpeech.QUEUE_ADD, null);

                                    }

                            }

                    }

                    else

                    {

                            m_DebugMsg += "ClientConnectThread is Null!! \n";

                    }


                    m_DebugMsgView.setText(m_DebugMsg.toCharArray(), 0, m_DebugMsg.length());

            }
```

```
        });


        // Create the Client Socket Connection Thread

        CreateClientConnection(m_ServerStaticIP, m_PortNumber);


        // Sets PhotoData array which holds

        m_PhotoData = m_WifiMessageHandler.GetBinaryData();

}
```

The TextToSpeechInit() Function

The TextToSpeechInitI() function initializes a new text to speech object variable m_TTS by setting the language to be spoken to English. The function does this by calling the m_TTS.setLanguage(Locale.US) function with the Locale.US value as an input parameter.

See Listing 6-9.

Listing 6-9. The TextToSpeechInit() function

```
void TextToSpeechInit()

{

        m_TTS = new TextToSpeech(MainActivity.this, new TextToSpeech.OnInitListener() {

                @Override

                public void onInit(int status) {

                    if(status == TextToSpeech.SUCCESS){

                        int result=m_TTS.setLanguage(Locale.US);

                        if(result==TextToSpeech.LANG_MISSING_DATA ||

                          result==TextToSpeech.LANG_NOT_SUPPORTED){

                          Log.e("error", "This Language is not supported");

                        }

                    }

                else
```

```
                    Log.e("error", "Initilization Failed!");

            }

        });

}
```

The LoadInPhoneNumber() Function

The LoadInPhoneNumber() function retrieves the emergency phone number from the shared preferences file by:

1. Retrieving the shared preferences settings for the Android application by calling the this.getSharedPreferences(m_GotchaCamPreferencesFile, 0) function with the filename that contains the settings for this application. The result is assigned to the settings variable.

2. Retrieving the string that represents the emergency phone number by calling the settings.getString(m_EmergencyPhoneNumberHandle, "None") function with the handle that the emergency phone number was stored under. The retrieved string is assigned to m_EmergencyPhoneNumber.

See Listing 6-10.

Listing 6-10. The LoadInPhoneNumber() Function

```
void LoadInPhoneNumber()

{

        SharedPreferences settings = this.getSharedPreferences(m_GotchaCamPreferencesFile, 0);

        m_EmergencyPhoneNumber = settings.getString(m_EmergencyPhoneNumberHandle, "None");

}
```

The HideKeyboard() Function

The HideKeyboard() function hides the keyboard after the user enters the emergency phone number into the phone text edit box by:

1. Retrieving the Android's InputMethodManager class object by calling the getSystemService(Context.INPUT_METHOD_SERVICE) function with the Context.INPUT_METHOD_SERVICE parameter.

2. Hiding the Android's keyboard from view by calling the hideSoftInputFromWindow(TargetView.getWindowToken(), 0) function from the InputMethodManager class that was retrieved in step 1.

See Listing 6-11.

Listing 6-11. The HideKeyboard Function

```
void HideKeyboard()

{

        View TargetView = this.getCurrentFocus();

        if (TargetView != null)

        {

                InputMethodManager imm =
(InputMethodManager)getSystemService(Context.INPUT_METHOD_SERVICE);

                imm.hideSoftInputFromWindow(TargetView.getWindowToken(), 0);

        }

}
```

The SavePhoneNumber() Function

The SavePhoneNumber() function saves the emergency phone number as a shared preference by:

1. Retrieving the shared preferences settings for this application by calling the this.getSharedPreferences(m_GotchaCamPreferencesFile, 0) function with the filename of the shared preferences. The returned value is assigned to the settings variable.

2. Retrieving the Editor class object for this group of shared preferences by calling the settings.edit() function and assigning the returned value to the editor variable.

3. Putting the emergency phone number string value into the shared preferences for this application by calling the editor.putString(m_EmergencyPhoneNumberHandle, m_EmergencyPhoneNumber) function. The first parameter is the handle that is used as an index to store and read back in the associated value. The second parameter is the emergency phone number.

4. Saving the changes to the shared preferences by calling the editor.commit() function.

See Listing 6-12.

Listing 6-12. The SavePhoneNumber() function

```
void SavePhoneNumber()

{

        SharedPreferences settings = this.getSharedPreferences(m_GotchaCamPreferencesFile, 0);

        SharedPreferences.Editor editor = settings.edit();
```

```
editor.putString(m_EmergencyPhoneNumberHandle, m_EmergencyPhoneNumber);

editor.commit();

}
```

The UpdateCommandTextView() Function

The UpdateCommandTextView() function updates the information settings window that displays the key settings for the GotchaCAM security system.

The function displays the following:

1. The alarm system status which is either on or off.

2. The emergency phone call out setting of the alarm system.

3. The emergency text message alert setting of the alarm system.

4. The surveillance status of the system which is either on or off.

5. The camera resolution that will be used to capture the image when the next surveillance or take photo command is executed.

6. The Android image storage setting.

7. The Motion Detection Accuracy setting.

8. The Motion Detection Threshold percent error setting that is used to determine the Motion Detection Threshold.

9. The minimum number of motions for the alarm to trip.

10. The false positive time interval in seconds.

See Listing 6-13.

Listing 6-13. The UpdateCommandTextView() function

```
void UpdateCommandTextView()

{

        String AlarmStatus = "";

        String CallOutStatus = "";

        String SurveillanceStatus = "";
```

```
// Get Current Camera Resolution and set text view

if (m_AlarmSet)

{

        AlarmStatus = "AlarmON";

}

else

{

        AlarmStatus = "AlarmOFF";

}


if (m_CallOutSet)

{

        CallOutStatus = "CallOutON";

}

else

{

        CallOutStatus = "CallOutOFF";

}


if (m_SurveillanceActive)

{

        SurveillanceStatus = "SurveilOn";

}

else

{

        SurveillanceStatus = "SurveilOff";

}


String Info = AlarmStatus + "\n" +
```

```
                    CallOutStatus + "\n" +

                    m_TextMessagesSetting + "\n" +

                    SurveillanceStatus + "\n" +

                    m_Resolution.toString() + "\n" +

                    m_AndroidStorage + "\n" +

                    "MDA: " + m_SADAccuracy + "\n" +

                    "MDT: " + m_SADThresholdPercentError + "\n" +

                    "MMAT: " + m_MinimumMotionsForAlarmTrip + "\n" +

                    "FPTI: " + m_FalsePositiveTimeInterval/1000;

         int length = Info.length();

         m_InfoTextView.setText(Info.toCharArray(), 0, length);

}
```

The InitExternalStorage() Function

The InitExternalStorage() function retrieves the directory that the images from the MT9D111 will be stored in.

The function does the following:

1. Tests if the storage is writable by calling the isExternalStorageWritable() function. Displays a message in the Debug Window with the result.

2. Retrieves and prints out to the debug window the directory path to the user's "pictures" directory.

3. The final path to the directory is retrieved by calling the GetAlbumStorageDir(Environment.DIRECTORY_PICTURES, m_AndroidPicsDirectory) function with the input parameters for the directory type which is the pictures directory and the album name which will be "CAMPics".

4. The final path is printed to the debug window.

See Listing 6-14.

Listing 6-14. The InitExternalStorage() function

```
void InitExternalStorage()

{

         // Test for External Storage and check if writable
```

```
        if (isExternalStorageWritable())

        {

                String Message = "External Storage is PRESENT and WRITABLE ...\n";

                AddDebugMessage(Message);

        }

        else

        {

                String Message = "External Storage is GONE or NOT Writable !!!! \n";

                AddDebugMessage(Message);

        }


        // Get the user's Pictures directory

        File PicsDir = GetExternalStorageDirectoryPath(Environment.DIRECTORY_PICTURES);

        String Path = "User's Picture Directory: " + PicsDir.getAbsolutePath() + " ...\n";

        AddDebugMessage(Path);


        // Get/Create Directory for  Camera pictures

        m_CameraDir = GetAlbumStorageDir(Environment.DIRECTORY_PICTURES, m_AndroidPicsDirectory);

        Path = "Camera Pics Directory: " + m_CameraDir.getAbsolutePath() + " ...\n";

        AddDebugMessage(Path);

}
```

The isExternalStorageWritable() Function

The isExternalStorageWritable() function determines if the external storage on the Android file system is writable by:

1. Getting the external storage state of the Android system by calling the Environment.getExternalStorageState() function.

2. If the result is equal to "MEDIA_MOUNTED" then we can save the images to storage.

See Listing 6-15.

Listing 6-15. The isExternalStorageWritable() function

```
public boolean isExternalStorageWritable()

{

        String state = Environment.getExternalStorageState();

        if (Environment.MEDIA_MOUNTED.equals(state))

        {

                return true;

        }

        return false;

}
```

The GetExternalStorageDirectoryPath() Function

The GetExternalStorageDirectoryPath() function gets the path of the type of directory input by the user.

See Listing 6-16.

Listing 6-16. The GetExternalStorageDirectoryPath() function

```
public File GetExternalStorageDirectoryPath(String DirectoryType)

{

        File Path = Environment.getExternalStoragePublicDirectory(DirectoryType);

        return Path;

}
```

The GetAlbumStorageDir() Function

The GetAlbumStorageDir() function creates and returns a new File object by:

1. Creating a new File class object using the input parameters of DirectoryType and AlbumName. This File object retrieves the system file path for the DirectoryType such as Pictures that is on the Android file system and adds on the AlbumName to the end of the path.

2. Attempting to create this new path by calling the file.mkdirs() function which makes all the directories in the path contained in the file variable from Step 1. Add a message to the Debug Window if the path could not be created.

See Listing 6-17.

Listing 6-17. The GetAlbumStorageDir() function

```
public File GetAlbumStorageDir(String DirectoryType, String AlbumName)

{

        // Get the directory for the user's album

        File file = new File(Environment.getExternalStoragePublicDirectory(DirectoryType), AlbumName);

        if (!file.mkdirs()) {

                Log.e(TAG, "External Storage Album Directory not created !!!!");

                String Error = "External Storage Album Directory not created !!!!\n";

                AddDebugMessage(Error);

        }

        return file;

}
```

The CreateClientConnection() Function

The CreateClientConnection() initiates the wifi connection from the Android to the CC3200 device by:

1. Creating a new WifiMessageHandler class with the current MainActivity class object as a parameter and assigning the result to m_WifiMessageHandler.

2. Creating a new Client class object by calling the Client(ServerStaticIP, PortNumber, m_WifiMessageHandler, this) function. The first parameter is the ip of the CC3200 server. The second parameter is the server port number. The third parameter is the wifi message handler for this application. The last parameter is the current instance of the MainActivity class. The new Client object is assigned to m_ClientConnectThread.

3. If the m_ClientConnectThread is not null then print out a message to the debug window indicating that the wifi connection is being started and start the client by calling the m_ClientConnectThread.start() function.

See Listing 6-18.

Listing 6-18. The CreateClientConnection() function

```
void CreateClientConnection(String ServerStaticIP, int PortNumber)

{
```

```
m_WifiMessageHandler = new WifiMessageHandler(this);

m_ClientConnectThread = new Client(ServerStaticIP, PortNumber, m_WifiMessageHandler, this);

if (m_ClientConnectThread != null)

{

        AddDebugMessage(TAG + ": Starting ClientConnectThread ...\n");

        m_ClientConnectThread.start();

}

}
```

The onOptionsItemSelected() Function

The onOptionsItemSelected() function is called when the user touches an element in the Android application's graphic user interface.

The onOptionsItemSelected() does the following:

1. If the group id of the item that the user has touched is 95 then call the LoadInAndroidImage(item) function which loads in the image file from the Android's storage that the user has selected.

2. If the user selects R.id.alarm_activate which is the menu item to activate the alarm then the SetAlarmStatus(true) function is called with the true parameter to turn on the security system. The UpdateCommandTextView() function is also called to update the information settings editbox with the new status of the alarm system. A short message is also displayed to confirm the selection by calling the Toast.makeText() function.

3. If the user selects R.id.alarm_deactivate which is the menu item to deactivate the alarm then the SetAlarmStatus(false) function is called with the false parameter to turn off the security system. The UpdateCommandTextView() function is called to update the information settings editbox with the new status of the alarm system. A message is also displayed confirming the user selection by calling the Toast.makeText() function.

4. If the user selects R.id.callout_on which is the menu item to turn on the emergency phone number call out then call the SetCallOutStatus(true) function with the true parameter to activate the call out feature. Update the information settings editbox by calling the UpdateCommandTextView() function. Display a message to the user that confirms the selection by calling the Toast.makeText() function.

5. If the user selects R.id.callout_off then the SetCallOutStatus(false) function is called with the false parameter which turns off the emergency phone call out feature. The UpdateCommandTextView() function is called to update the information settings editbox. Display a message to the user that confirms the selection by calling the Toast.makeText() function.

6. If the user selects to turn emergency text message alerts off which maps to the R.id.notext value then call the SetTextMessageStatus(TextMessageSetting.TEXT_OFF) function with the value to turn off text messaging. The UpdateCommandTextView() function updates the

information setting editbox. A Message is displayed that confirms that text message alerts have been turned off by calling the Toast.makeText() function.

7. If the user turns on the emergency text message alerts which maps to the R.id.text_only value then call the SetTextMessageStatus(TextMessageSetting.TEXT_ON) with the TEXT_ON parameter to turn on the text messaging system. The information settings edit box is updated by calling the UpdateCommandTextView() function. A confirmation message indicating that emergency text messaging alerts has been turned on is displayed by calling the Toast.makeText() function.

8. If the item selected has an id of R.id.qqvga which is the QQVGA resolution from the menu then call the SetCameraResolution(Resolution.QQVGA) function with the QQVGA parameter to actually set the camera resolution. The information settings window is updated by calling the UpdateCommandTextView() function.

9. If the item selected has an id of R.id.qvga which is the QVGA resolution from the menu then call the SetCameraResolution(Resolution.QVGA) function with the QVGA parameter to actually change the camera resolution. The information settings window is updated by calling the UpdateCommandTextView() function.

10. If the item selected has an id of R.id.vga which is the VGA resolution from the menu then call the SetCameraResolution(Resolution.VGA) function with the VGA parameter. Update the information settings edit box by calling the UpdateCommandTextView() function.

11. If the item selected has an id of R.id.surveillance_on which turns on the constant camera streaming of images then call the ProcessSurveillanceSelection(true) function with the true parameter to actually turn on the surveillance. The information settings window is updated by calling the UpdateCommandTextView() function. A message is displayed confirming the user's selection by calling the Toast.makeText() function.

12. If the item selected has an id of R.id.surveillance_off which turns off the constant camera streaming of the images then call the ProcessSurveillanceSelection(false) function with the false parameter to actually turn off the surveillance. The information settings window is updated by calling the UpdateCommandTextView() function. A message is displayed confirming the user's selection by calling the Toast.makeText() function.

13. If the item selected has an id of R.id.loadandroidimage which loads and displays a menu of image files available for viewing then call the ProcessLoadJpgImagesAndroid(item) with the menu item object that the user touches to actually load in and display the list of images.

14. If the item selected has an id of R.id.androidstorageyes which turns on the saving of incoming images to the Android's file system then assign AndroidStorage.StoreYes to m_AndroidStorage. The information settings window is updated by calling the UpdateCommandTextView() function. A message is displayed confirming the user's selection by calling the Toast.makeText() function.

15. If the item selected has an id of R.id.androidstorageno which turns off the saving of incoming images to the Android's file system then assign AndroidStorage.StoreNo to m_AndroidStorage. The information settings window is updated by calling the UpdateCommandTextView() function. A message is displayed confirming the user's selection by calling the Toast.makeText() function.

16. If the item selected has an id of R.id.motionhigh then set the SAD motion detection method to calculate the SAD value for every pixel of the image by assigning 1 to m_SADAccuracy. The information settings window is updated by calling the UpdateCommandTextView() function.

A message is displayed confirming the user's selection by calling the Toast.makeText() function.

17. If the item selected has an id of R.id.motionmedium then set the SAD motion detection method to calculate the SAD value for every fourth pixel by assigning 4 to m_SADAccuracy. The information settings window is updated by calling the UpdateCommandTextView() function. A message is displayed confirming the user's selection by calling the Toast.makeText() function.

18. If the item selected has an id of R.id.motionlow then set the SAD motion detection method to calculate the SAD value for every 8 pixel by assigning 8 to m_SADAccuracy. The information settings window is updated by calling the UpdateCommandTextView() function. A message is displayed confirming the user's selection by calling the Toast.makeText() function.

19. If the item selected has an id of R.id.fivepercent then set the percent error for the SAD threshold calculation to 0.05. Update the information settings edit box and display a confirmation message.

20. If the item selected has an id of R.id.tenpercent then set the percent error for the SAD threshold calculation to 0.10. Update the information settings edit box and display a confirmation message.

21. If the item selected has an id of R.id.fifteenpercent then set the percent error for the SAD threshold calculation to 0.15. Update the information settings edit box and display a confirmation message.

22. If the item selected has an id of R.id.twentypercent then set the percent error for the SAD threshold calculation to 0.20. Update the information settings edit box and display a confirmation message.

23. If the item selected has an id of R.id.twentyfivepercent then set the percent error for the SAD threshold calculation to 0.25. Update the information settings edit box and display a confirmation message.

24. If the item selected has an id of R.id.fiveseconds then set the false positive time interval to 5000 milliseconds or 5 seconds. Update the information settings edit box and display a confirmation message.

25. If the item selected has an id of R.id.tenseconds then set the false positive time interval to 10000 milliseconds or 10 seconds. Update the information settings edit box and display a confirmation message.

26. If the item selected has an id of R.id.fifteenseconds then set the false positive interval to 15000 milliseconds or 15 seconds. Update the information settings edit box and display a confirmation message.

27. If the item selected has an id of R.id.twentyseconds then set the false positive time interval to 20000 milliseconds or 20 seconds. Update the information settings edit box and display a confirmation message.

28. If the item selected has an id of R.id.twentyfive then set the false positive time interval to 25000 milliseconds or 25 seconds. Update the information settings edit box and display a confirmation message.

29. If the item selected has an id of R.id.one then set the minimum number of motions that are needed to trip the alarm to 1. Update the information settings edit box and display a confirmation message.

30. If the item selected has an id of R.id.threemotions then set the minimum number of motions that are needed to trip the alarm to 3. Update the information settings edit box and display a confirmation message.

31. If the item selected has an id of R.id.fivemotions then set the minimum number of motions that are needed to trip the alarm to 5. Update the information settings edit box and display a confirmation message.

32. If the item selected has an id of R.id.eightmotions then set the minimum number of motions that are needed to trip the alarm to 8. Update the information settings edit box and display a confirmation message.

33. If the item selected has an id of R.id.elevenmotions then set the minimum number of motions that are needed to trip the alarm to 11. Update the information settings edit box and display a confirmation message.

See Listing 6-19.

Listing 6-19. The onOptionsItemSelected() function

```
@Override

public boolean onOptionsItemSelected(MenuItem item)

{

        // Process file selection located on Android

        if (item.getGroupId() == 95)

        {

                LoadInAndroidImage(item);

                return true;

        }


        // Handle item selection

        switch (item.getItemId()) {


                /////////////////////// Alarm Activation

                case R.id.alarm_activate:
```

```
                SetAlarmStatus(true);

                UpdateCommandTextView();

                Toast.makeText(this, "Alarm Activated !!!", Toast.LENGTH_LONG).show();

                return true;


        case R.id.alarm_deactivate:

                SetAlarmStatus(false);

                UpdateCommandTextView();

                Toast.makeText(this, "Alarm Deactivated !!!", Toast.LENGTH_LONG).show();

                return true;


        /////////////////////// Alarm Emergency Phone Callout
case R.id.callout_on:

        SetCallOutStatus(true);

        UpdateCommandTextView();

        Toast.makeText(this, "Call Out Activated !!!", Toast.LENGTH_LONG).show();

    return true;


case R.id.callout_off:

        SetCallOutStatus(false);

        UpdateCommandTextView();

        Toast.makeText(this, "Call Out Deactivated !!!", Toast.LENGTH_LONG).show();

    return true;


/////////////////////// Text messages
case R.id.notext:

        SetTextMessageStatus(TextMessageSetting.TEXT_OFF);

        UpdateCommandTextView();

        Toast.makeText(this, "Text Message Alerts Turned Off !!!", Toast.LENGTH_LONG).show();
```

```
        return true;


case R.id.text_only:

        SetTextMessageStatus(TextMessageSetting.TEXT_ON);

        UpdateCommandTextView();

        Toast.makeText(this, "Text Message Alerts Activated !!!", Toast.LENGTH_LONG).show();

    return true;


/////////////////////// Resolution

case R.id.qqvga:

        SetCameraResolution(Resolution.QQVGA);

        UpdateCommandTextView();

        return true;


case R.id.qvga:

        SetCameraResolution(Resolution.QVGA);

        UpdateCommandTextView();

        return true;


case R.id.vga:

        SetCameraResolution(Resolution.VGA);

        UpdateCommandTextView();

        return true;


////////////////////////// Surveillance

case R.id.surveillance_on:

        ProcessSurveillanceSelection(true);

        UpdateCommandTextView();

        Toast.makeText(this, "Surveillance Turned On !!!", Toast.LENGTH_LONG).show();
```

```
            return true;


        case R.id.surveillance_off:

            ProcessSurveillanceSelection(false);

            UpdateCommandTextView();

            Toast.makeText(this, "Surveillance Turned Off !!!", Toast.LENGTH_LONG).show();

            return true;


        ///////////////////////////// Load Stored Image

        case R.id.loadandroidimage:

            ProcessLoadJpgImagesAndroid(item);

            return true;


        ///////////////////////////// Android Storage

        case R.id.androidstorageyes:

            m_AndroidStorage = AndroidStorage.StoreYes;

            UpdateCommandTextView();

            Toast.makeText(this, "Images will be saved to Android Storage", Toast.LENGTH_LONG).show();

            return true;


        case R.id.androidstorageno:

            m_AndroidStorage = AndroidStorage.StoreNo;

            UpdateCommandTextView();

            Toast.makeText(this, "Images will NOT be saved to Android Storage",
Toast.LENGTH_LONG).show();

            return true;


        ///////////////////////////// Motion Detection Accuracy

        case R.id.motionhigh:

            m_SADAccuracy = 1; // Monitor change for every pixel of image.
```

```
        UpdateCommandTextView();

        Toast.makeText(this, "Motion Detection Accuracy Set To High", Toast.LENGTH_LONG).show();

        return true;


    case R.id.motionmedium:

        m_SADAccuracy = 4; // Monitor change for every 4th pixel of image.

        UpdateCommandTextView();

        Toast.makeText(this, "Motion Detection Accuracy Set To Medium",
Toast.LENGTH_LONG).show();

        return true;


    case R.id.motionlow:

        m_SADAccuracy = 8;  // Monitor change for every 8th pixel of image.

        UpdateCommandTextView();

        Toast.makeText(this, "Motion Detection Accuracy Set To Low", Toast.LENGTH_LONG).show();

        return true;


    /////////////////// Set Threshold Percent Error
    case R.id.fivepercent:

        m_SADThresholdPercentError = 0.05;

        UpdateCommandTextView();

        Toast.makeText(this, "Motion Detection Tolerance set to 5%", Toast.LENGTH_SHORT).show();

        return true;


    case R.id.tenpercent:

        m_SADThresholdPercentError = 0.10;

        UpdateCommandTextView();

        Toast.makeText(this, "Motion Detection Tolerance set to 10%", Toast.LENGTH_SHORT).show();

        return true;
```

```
case R.id.fifteenpercent:

    m_SADThresholdPercentError = 0.15;

    UpdateCommandTextView();

    Toast.makeText(this, "Motion Detection Tolerance set to 15%", Toast.LENGTH_SHORT).show();

    return true;


case R.id.twentypercent:

    m_SADThresholdPercentError = 0.20;

    UpdateCommandTextView();

    Toast.makeText(this, "Motion Detection Tolerance set to 20%", Toast.LENGTH_SHORT).show();

    return true;


case R.id.twentyfivepercent:

    m_SADThresholdPercentError = 0.25;

    UpdateCommandTextView();

    Toast.makeText(this, "Motion Detection Tolerance set to 25%", Toast.LENGTH_SHORT).show();

    return true;


// False Positive

case R.id.fiveseconds:

    m_FalsePositiveTimeInterval = 1000 * 5;

    UpdateCommandTextView();

    Toast.makeText(this, "False Positive Time Interval Set To " + m_FalsePositiveTimeInterval/1000 +
" Seconds", Toast.LENGTH_SHORT).show();

    return true;


case R.id.tenseconds:

    m_FalsePositiveTimeInterval = 1000 * 10;

    UpdateCommandTextView();
```

```
                Toast.makeText(this, "False Positive Time Interval Set To " + m_FalsePositiveTimeInterval/1000 +
" Seconds", Toast.LENGTH_SHORT).show();

                return true;



        case R.id.fifteenseconds:

                m_FalsePositiveTimeInterval = 1000 * 15;

                UpdateCommandTextView();

                Toast.makeText(this, "False Positive Time Interval Set To " + m_FalsePositiveTimeInterval/1000 +
" Seconds", Toast.LENGTH_SHORT).show();

                return true;



        case R.id.twentyseconds:

                m_FalsePositiveTimeInterval = 1000 * 20;

                UpdateCommandTextView();

                Toast.makeText(this, "False Positive Time Interval Set To " + m_FalsePositiveTimeInterval/1000 +
" Seconds", Toast.LENGTH_SHORT).show();

                return true;



        case R.id.twentyfive:

                m_FalsePositiveTimeInterval = 1000 * 25;

                UpdateCommandTextView();

                Toast.makeText(this, "False Positive Time Interval Set To " + m_FalsePositiveTimeInterval/1000 +
" Seconds", Toast.LENGTH_SHORT).show();

                return true;



        // Minimum Motions for Alarm Trip
        case R.id.one:

                m_MinimumMotionsForAlarmTrip = 1;

                UpdateCommandTextView();

                Toast.makeText(this, "Minimum Number of Motions Needed for Tripping Alarm set to " +
m_MinimumMotionsForAlarmTrip, Toast.LENGTH_SHORT).show();

                return true;
```

```
case R.id.threemotions:

    m_MinimumMotionsForAlarmTrip = 3;

    UpdateCommandTextView();

    Toast.makeText(this, "Minimum Number of Motions Needed for Tripping Alarm set to " +
m_MinimumMotionsForAlarmTrip, Toast.LENGTH_SHORT).show();

    return true;


case R.id.fivemotions:

    m_MinimumMotionsForAlarmTrip = 5;

    UpdateCommandTextView();

    Toast.makeText(this, "Minimum Number of Motions Needed for Tripping Alarm set to " +
m_MinimumMotionsForAlarmTrip, Toast.LENGTH_SHORT).show();

    return true;


case R.id.eightmotions:

    m_MinimumMotionsForAlarmTrip = 8;

    UpdateCommandTextView();

    Toast.makeText(this, "Minimum Number of Motions Needed for Tripping Alarm set to " +
m_MinimumMotionsForAlarmTrip, Toast.LENGTH_SHORT).show();

    return true;


case R.id.elevenmotions:

    m_MinimumMotionsForAlarmTrip = 11;

    UpdateCommandTextView();

    Toast.makeText(this, "Minimum Number of Motions Needed for Tripping Alarm set to " +
m_MinimumMotionsForAlarmTrip, Toast.LENGTH_SHORT).show();

    return true;


default:

    return super.onOptionsItemSelected(item);
```

```
        }

    }
```

The LoadInAndroidImage() Function

The LoadInAndroidImage() function loads in the file selected by the user and displays the image on the Android user interface.

The function does the following:

1. Continues processing the selected menu item only if it is located on the Android file system as indicated by the item's group id being equal to the Android file group ID.

2. Gets the filename from the menu item by converting the menu item's title into a string.

3. Loads the image data from the file into the m_PhotoData variable by calling the LoadImageDataAndroid(m_CameraDir, filename) function with the parameters for the directory and the filename of the file in the directory to load.

4. Finally, the file image data is converted into a viewable format and displayed on the Android device by calling the LoadJpegPhotoUI(m_PhotoData) function with the JPEG picture data.

See Listing 6-20.

Listing 6-20. The LoadInAndroidImage() function

```
void LoadInAndroidImage(MenuItem item)

{

        String filename = "";


        if (item.getGroupId() == m_AndroidFileGroupID)

        {

                filename = item.getTitle().toString();

                Log.e("Main Activity", "Android image File Selected = " + "'" + filename + "'");


                LoadImageDataAndroid(m_CameraDir, filename);

                LoadJpegPhotoUI(m_PhotoData);

        }

    }
```

The LoadImageDataAndroid() Function

The LoadImageDataAndroid() loads in the image data from the file by:

1. Creating a new File object using the directory the file is in and the filename.

2. Creating a buffered input stream using the File object from step 1 and reading in all the file data and storing it in the m_PhotoData array variable.

See Listing 6-21.

Listing 6-21. The LoadImageDataAndroid() function

```
void LoadImageDataAndroid(File Dir, String filename)

{

        // Loads binary image data from the filename located in Dir directory from Android

        // and puts it into the m_PhotoData array used to hold the current image data being

        // displayed on Android


        // Open File to write out image data

        File file = new File(Dir, filename);


        if (file != null)

        {

                Log.e("MainActivity", "Android Image File path constructed ....");

                Log.e("MainActivity", "Directory = " + Dir);

                Log.e("MainActivity", "Filename = " + filename);

        }


        InputStream iStream = null;

        int InputByte = 0;

        int Index = 0;


        try
```

```
        {

                iStream = new BufferedInputStream(new FileInputStream(file));

                while (InputByte >= 0)

                {

                        InputByte = iStream.read();

                        if (InputByte != -1)

                        {

                                m_PhotoData[Index] = (byte)InputByte;

                                Index++;

                        }

                }

        }

        catch (IOException e)

        {

                Log.e("MainActivity", "Cannot load image data from Android...");

        }

}
```

The LoadJpegPhotoUI() Function

The LoadJpegPhotoUI() function displays a JPEG image on the Android device's user interface based on the input JpegData.

The function does the following:

1. The data in the JpegData byte array is decoded into a bitmap image. This is done by calling the BitmapFactory.decodeByteArray(JpegData, offset, length) function with the image data, the offset from the beginning of the array to where the image data starts and the length of the data that forms the image.

2. The ImageView window that will hold the image is found by calling the findViewById(R.id.imageView1) function with the resource id of the window we want to put the image in.

3. If the image was successfully decoded then the image is put into the window by calling the ImageView.setImageBitmap(BM) function with the bitmap image generated from the JPEG data from Step 1. The current bitmap image is set to the previous bitmap image by assigning m_BitmapPrevious the value from m_BitmapCurrent. The current incoming bitmap that was just decoded is assigned to m_BitmapCurrent. If the alarm is set then calculate the sum of

the absolute difference between the previous bitmap and the current bitmap by calling the SumAbsoluteDifferenceCalculation(m_BitmapPrevious, m_BitmapCurrent) function with references to the previous and current bitmap images and assign the returned value to m_SAD.

4. If the image from Step 1 is null which means that the decoding failed then issue an error in the log window by calling the Log.e() function.

See Listing 6-22.

Listing 6-22. The LoadJpegPhotoUI() function

```
void LoadJpegPhotoUI(byte[] JpegData)

{

        /*

                        public static Bitmap decodeByteArray (byte[] data, int offset, int length)

                        Added in API level 1


                        Decode an immutable bitmap from the specified byte array.


                        Parameters:

                        data        byte array of compressed image data

                        offset      offset into imageData for where the decoder should begin parsing.

                        length      the number of bytes, beginning at offset, to parse


                        Returns:

                        The decoded bitmap, or null if the image could not be decoded.

        */


        Bitmap BM = null;


        int offset = 0;

        int length = JpegData.length;
```

```
BM = BitmapFactory.decodeByteArray(JpegData, offset, length);


ImageView ImageView = (ImageView) findViewById(R.id.imageView1);

if (BM != null)

{

        ImageView.setImageBitmap(BM);


        // Set Current and Previous Bitmaps

        m_BitmapPrevious = m_BitmapCurrent;

        m_BitmapCurrent = BM;


        if (m_AlarmSet)

        {

                // Calculate SAD between this image and previous image

                m_SAD = SumAbsoluteDifferenceCalculation(m_BitmapPrevious, m_BitmapCurrent);

        }

}

else

{

        Log.e("MainActivity", "ImageView Bitmap Creation Failed!!!");

        AddDebugMessage(TAG + ": ImageView Bitmap Creation Failed !!!\n");

}

}
```

The SetAlarmStatus() Function

The SetAlarmStatus() turns on or turns off the security system by doing the following:

1. If the input parameter to the function is true then turn on the alarm and notify the user through the Android's text to speech function.

2. If the input parameter to the function is false then turn off the alarm and notify the user through the Android's text to speech function. Reset the variables related to the emergency

phone call out. Reset the number of detected motions to 0. Reset the emergency message sent flag. Reset the SAD calibration variables.

See Listing 6-23.

Listing 6-23. The SetAlarmStatus function

```
void SetAlarmStatus(boolean status)

{

        if (status == true)

        {

                m_AlarmSet = true;

                m_TTS.speak("Activateing Alarm", TextToSpeech.QUEUE_ADD, null);

        }

        else

        {

                m_AlarmSet = false;

                m_TTS.speak("DeActivating Alarm", TextToSpeech.QUEUE_ADD, null);


                // Reset Callout Variables

                m_CallOutDone = false;

                m_EmergencyMessageDone = false;

                m_AlarmTripped = false;


                // Reset number of detected motions to 0

                m_NumberMotionsDetected = 0;


                // Reset Emergency Message Sent flag

                m_TextMessageSent = false;


                // Reset SAD Calibration Variables
```

```
        m_SADCount = 0;

        m_SADCalcThreshold = 0;

        m_SADCalibrationDone = false;

        m_SADHighest = 0;

    }

}
```

The SetCallOutStatus() Function

The SetCallOutStatus() function does the following:

1. Activates the emergency cell phone call out if the input parameter status is true. Also gives a vocalized notification that the call out has been activated.

2. Deactivates the emergency cell phone call out if the input parameter status is false. Also gives a vocalized notification that the call out has been turned off.

See Listing 6-24.

Listing 6-24. The SetCallOutStatus() function

```
void SetCallOutStatus(boolean status)

{

        if (status == true)

        {

                m_CallOutSet = true;

                m_TTS.speak("Activating Emergency Call Out", TextToSpeech.QUEUE_ADD, null);

        }

        else

        {

                m_CallOutSet = false;

                m_TTS.speak("DeActivating Emergency Call Out", TextToSpeech.QUEUE_ADD, null);

        }

}
```

The SetTextMessageStatus() Function

The SetTextMessageStatus() function does the following:

1. Sets the emergency text message alert setting to the one provided by the user.

2. Notifies the user that the emergency text message alert setting has been changed by issuing a vocal alert using the Android text to speech system.

See Listing 6-25.

Listing 6-25. The SetTextMessageStatus() function

```
void SetTextMessageStatus(TextMessageSetting Setting)

{

        m_TextMessagesSetting = Setting;

        m_TTS.speak("Emergency Text Messages Set to " + m_TextMessagesSetting,
TextToSpeech.QUEUE_ADD, null);

}
```

The SetCameraResolution() Function

The SetCameraResolution() function:

1. Sets the resolution of the MT9D111 camera on the next image capture.

2. Displays a message that notifies the user that the resolution has been changed by calling the Toast.makeText() function.

See Listing 6-26.

Listing 6-26. The SetCameraResolution() function

```
void SetCameraResolution(Resolution Res)

{

        m_Resolution = Res;

        Toast.makeText(this, "Resolution set to " + m_Resolution, Toast.LENGTH_LONG).show();

}
```

The ProcessSurveillanceSelection() Function

The ProcessSurveillanceSelection() function activates or deactivates the surveillance system based on the input parameter.

The function does the following:

1. If surveillance is already on and the user is trying to turn on surveillance then do nothing since surveillance is already on and exit the function.

2. If the user selects to turn surveillance on then activate the surveillance, reset the surveillance frame number and execute the SendTakePhotoCommand() function in order to perform a "Take Photo" command to begin the surveillance.

3. If the user selects to turn surveillance off then the surveillance is turned off.

See Listing 6-27.

Listing 6-27. The ProcessSurveillanceSelection() function

```
void ProcessSurveillanceSelection(boolean Activated)

{

        if (m_SurveillanceActive && Activated)

        {

                // surveillance is already activated so do nothing

                return;

        }



        // If surveillance set to active

        if (Activated)

        {

                // Surveillance is set to on.

                m_SurveillanceActive = true;



                // Disable "Take Photo" button while video surveillance is active

                m_TakePhotoButtonActive = false;
```

```
                    // Reset Surveillance Frame Number

                    m_SurveillanceFrameNumber = 0;


                    // Send TakePhoto Command

                    SendTakePhotoCommand();

            }

        else

            {

                    m_SurveillanceActive = false;

            }

    }
```

The ProcessLoadJpgImagesAndroid() Function

The ProcessLoadJpgImagesAndroid() function loads in the filenames of the JPEG files located in the directory we specifically created for the camera images for our intruder alarm system.

The function does the following:

1. Gets the submenu from the input menuitem input parameter by assigning to the variable submenu1 the result from the menuitem.getSubMenu() function call.

2. Retrieves a list of filenames in the directory we created for storing camera images by calling the m_CameraDir.list() function.

3. Assign the number of files in the directory to the m_NumberFileNames variable.

4. Clear all the entries in the "Load JPEG Image From Android" menu that lists the JPEG files in the camera image storage directory we previously defined by calling the submenu1.clear() function.

5. For each filename in the m_AndroidFileNames String array test to see if the filename's extension indicates that it is a JPEG file by calling the IsFileJPEG(m_AndroidFileNames[i]) function on each element in the array.

6. If the filename has a .jpg extension then add this filename to the "Load JPEG Image From Android" sub menu by calling the submenu1.add(m_AndroidFileGroupID, m_AndroidFileItemID, i, m_AndroidFileNames[i]) function with input parameters that identify this entry as located on the Android file system and the name of the image file.

See Listing 6-28.

Lisring 6-28. The ProcessLoadJpgImagesAndroid() function

```java
void ProcessLoadJpgImagesAndroid(MenuItem menuitem)
{
        Log.e("MainActivity","In ProcessLoadJpgImagesAndroid");

        SubMenu submenu1 = menuitem.getSubMenu();


        // Load Android JPG directory

        m_AndroidFileNames = m_CameraDir.list();

        m_NumberFileNames = m_AndroidFileNames.length;


        if (submenu1 != null)

        {
                // Add files  Here.

                submenu1.clear();

                for (int i = 0; i < m_NumberFileNames; i++)

                {
                        if (IsFileJPEG(m_AndroidFileNames[i]))

                        {
                                submenu1.add(m_AndroidFileGroupID, m_AndroidFileItemID, i,
m_AndroidFileNames[i]);

                        }

                }

        }

        else

        {
                Log.e("MainActivity", "ERROR, Can not get SubMenu");

        }

}
```

The IsFileJPEG() Function

The IsFileJPEG() function returns true if the input filename extension is ".jpg" and false otherwise.

The function does the following:

1. Find the starting position of the filename extension by calling the filename.indexOf('.') function. The filename variable is the input string parameter.

2. Get the substring of the filename starting at one position after the position of the "." which will be the filename extension.

3. Convert this substring to lower case.

4. Trim this substring of any trailing whitespace characters such as spaces, new line characters, or control characters.

5. Compare this substring to "jpg". If there is a match return true to indicate that a JPEG file has been found. Otherwise, return false.

See Listing 6-29

Listing 6-29. The IsFileJPEG function

```
boolean IsFileJPEG(String filename)

{

        boolean ValidExtension = false;

        String Extension = filename;

        String ExtensionProcessed = "";

        String ExtensionTrimmed = "";


        int indexdot = filename.indexOf('.');

        int start = indexdot + 1;


        if (indexdot > 0)

        {

                ExtensionProcessed = Extension.substring(start);

                String LowerCaseExtensionProcessed = ExtensionProcessed.toLowerCase();

                ExtensionTrimmed = LowerCaseExtensionProcessed.trim();
```

```
                    int result = ExtensionTrimmed.compareTo("jpg");



                    if (result == 0)

                    {

                            ValidExtension = true;

                    }

            }



            return ValidExtension;

}
```

The run() Function

The run() function is called from another separate process or thread such as the Client class or the WifiMessageHandler class. The run() function is actually executed by calling the m_MainActivity.runOnUiThread(m_MainActivity) function with the MainActivity class object as the input parameter.

The run() function does the following:

1. If text data has been received and needs to be processed then call the ReceiveDisplayTextData() function. This is currently not used in the alarm system but serves as a template as to how you would process incoming text data from the CC3200.

2. If debug messages were added in other threads then update the debug message window to show these new messages and play a sound to notify the user that there are new messages in the debug window.

3. If the size of an incoming image needs to be processed then call the ProcessGetImageSizeCallback() function to process the image size.

4. If the data of the incoming image needs to be processed then do the following:

    1. Display the incoming image by calling the LoadJpegPhotoUI(m_PhotoData) function with the image data held in m_PhotoData.

    2. If surveillance is active then:

        1. Disable the "Take Photo" button by calling the m_TakePhotoButton.setEnabled(false) function with the input parameter of false.

        2. If the surveillance sound effects are on then play a sound effect to indicate that a new image has been received.

        3. Increase the surveillance frame number and print it to the debug message window.

172

4. If the alarm has been set and the SAD motion calibration has been done then print the SAD debug information to the debug message window. Check for movement by calling the MovementProcessing() function. Print out the number of motions detected to the debug window. If the alarm has been tripped then do the following:

1. Print out an "alarm tripped" message to the debug window.

2. Process the emergency phone callout function by calling the CheckProcessCallout() function.

3. Process the emergency text message alert function by calling the CheckProcessTextMessages() function.

4. If movement has been detected and the user has chosen to save images then call the SavePicJPEG() function to save the current image frame to the Android's storage system.

5. If the alarm has been set but SAD Calibration has not been done then calculate the SAD threshold by calling the CalculateSADThresHold() function. Print a notification message that the SAD calibration is being done to the debug message window.

6. Continue the surveillance by taking another picture with the MT9D111 camera and sending it to the Android device by calling the SendTakePhotoCommand() function.

3. If surveillance is not active then if the user has chosen to store an incoming image then call the SavePicJPEG() function to save the image to the Android's storage. The return value is the filename that the image has been stored under and this is printed out to the debug message window. Set the "Take Photo" button to active by setting the m_TakePhotoButtonActive variable to true. Play a notification sound effect that a new image has been returned from the CC3200 and has been displayed on the Android.

5. Set the state of the "Take Photo" button based on the value of m_TakePhotoButtonActive.

See Listing 6-30.

Listing 6-30. The run() function

```
public void run()

{

        if (m_RecieveTextDataCallBackDone)

        {

                ReceiveDisplayTextData();

                m_RecieveTextDataCallBackDone = false;

        }

        else

        if (m_RefreshMessageWindows)
```

```
        {
                m_DebugMsgView.setText(m_DebugMsg.toCharArray(), 0, m_DebugMsg.length());

                m_Alert2SFX.PlaySound(false);

                m_RefreshMessageWindows = false;

        }

else

if(m_TakePhotoCallbackDone)

{
                if (m_TakePhotoState == TakePhotoCallbackState.GetImageSize)

                {
                        m_TakePhotoCallbackDone = false;

                        ProcessGetImageSizeCallback();

                }

                else

                if (m_TakePhotoState == TakePhotoCallbackState.GetImageData)

                {
                        // Display New Photo received from the Arduino after pressing the

                        m_TakePhotoCallbackDone = false;

                        LoadJpegPhotoUI(m_PhotoData);


                        if (m_SurveillanceActive)

                        {
                                m_TakePhotoButton.setEnabled(false);

                                if (m_SurveillanceSFX)

                                {
                                        m_Alert1SFX.PlaySound(false);

                                }

                                m_SurveillanceFrameNumber++;

                                m_DebugMsg = "";
```

```
m_DebugMsg += "Frame Number: " + m_SurveillanceFrameNumber + "\n";

if (m_AlarmSet && m_SADCalibrationDone)

{

        m_DebugMsg += "SAD Value: " + m_SAD + "\n";

        m_DebugMsg += "SAD Threshold: " + m_SADThreshold + "\n";

        boolean MovementDetected = MovementProcessing();

        m_DebugMsg+= "Motions Detected: " +
m_NumberMotionsDetected + "\n";

        if (m_AlarmTripped)

        {

                m_DebugMsg+= "ALARM TRIPPED!!!!\n";

                CheckProcessCallout();

                CheckProcessTextMessages();

                if (MovementDetected)

                {

                        m_DebugMsg += "***Movement Detected\n";

                        m_SurveillanceFileName = "";

                        if (m_AndroidStorage ==
AndroidStorage.StoreYes)

                        {

                                SavePicJPEG();

                                m_DebugMsg += "File Name: " +
m_SurveillanceFileName + "\n";

                        }

                }

        }

}
else
if (m_AlarmSet && !m_SADCalibrationDone)

{

        // Perform SAD Noise calibration
```

```
                                CalculateSADThresHold();

                                m_DebugMsg += "Performing SAD Calibration ...\n";

                        }

                        m_DebugMsg += "\n\n\n\n";

                        m_DebugMsgView.setText(m_DebugMsg.toCharArray(), 0,
m_DebugMsg.length());

                        // Send another take photo command to CC3200

                        SendTakePhotoCommand();

                }
                else
                {

                        // If surveillance is not active and storage is yes

                        // then store image on Android

                        m_SurveillanceFileName = "";

                        if (m_AndroidStorage == AndroidStorage.StoreYes)

                        {

                                String filename = SavePicJPEG();

                                m_DebugMsg+= "File Name: " + filename + "\n";

                                m_DebugMsgView.setText(m_DebugMsg.toCharArray(), 0,
m_DebugMsg.length());

                        }

                        m_TakePhotoButtonActive = true;

                        m_Alert2SFX.PlaySound(true);

                }
        }
}
else
{

        // Error

        Log.e(TAG, "RUN:: ERROR IN RUN() ... No callback executed !!!!");
```

```
        }


        // Set Take Photo Button active state

        if (m_TakePhotoButtonActive == true)

        {

                m_TakePhotoButton.setEnabled(true);

        }

        else

        {

                m_TakePhotoButton.setEnabled(false);

        }

}
```

The ReceiveDisplayTextData() Function

The ReceiveDisplayTextData() function reads in the text data that was just sent from the CC3200 to the Android device over wifi and does the following:

1. The incoming text data is retrieved by calling the m_WifiMessageHandler.GetStringData() function and the value is stored in the Data variable.

2. The text is then stripped of whitespace characters by calling the Data.trim() function and the result is assigned to the DataTrimmed variable.

3. The text is then written to the LogCat window in the Android IDE by calling the Log() function.

4. The text is also written to the debug message window.

See Listing 6-31.

Listing 6-31. The ReceiveDisplayTextData() function

```
void ReceiveDisplayTextData()

{

        String Data = m_WifiMessageHandler.GetStringData();

        String DataTrimmed = Data.trim();
```

```
// Debug Print Outs

Log.e(TAG, "Returned Text Data = " + DataTrimmed);

m_DebugMsg = "";

AddDebugMessage(TAG + ": Returned Text Data = " + DataTrimmed + "\n");
```

}

The ProcessGetImageSizeCallback() Function

The ProcessGetImageSizeCallback() function processes the image size data by doing the following:

1. The incoming text data is retrieved from the WifiMessageHandler class.

2. The data is then trimmed of whitespace characters.

3. The trimmed text data is then converted to an integer and assigned to the m_PhotoSize variable.

4. Add a message to the debug window displaying the size of the incoming image.

5. Send the command to the CC3200 to transmit the actual image data to the Android device by calling the SendGetImageDataCommand() function.

See Listing 6-32.

Listing 6-32. The ProcessGetImageSizeCallback() function

```
void ProcessGetImageSizeCallback()

{

        String Data = m_WifiMessageHandler.GetStringData();

        String DataTrimmed = Data.trim();


        m_PhotoSize = Integer.parseInt(DataTrimmed);


        // Debug Print Outs

        AddDebugMessage("RUN:: Returned Image Size = " + m_PhotoSize + "\n");

        SendGetImageDataCommand();

}
```

The SendGetImageDataCommand() Function

The SendGetImageDataCommand() function sends the command to retrieve the image data to the CC3200 over wifi by doing the following:

1. Resets the data structures in the wifi message handler that is used to process incoming wifi data.

2. Sets the binary data length that is to be received to the size of the expected binary image data.

3. Set the command in the wifi message handler to "GetImageData". This command string will be used to process the incoming data.

4. If there is a wifi connection between the Android device and the CC3200 then disable the "Take Photo" button and send that actual command to the CC3200 by calling the m_ClientConnectThread.write(Command.getBytes()) function with the command string converted to an array of bytes. A message is printed to the debug message window notifying the user that the "GetImageData" command has been sent.

See Listing 6-33.

Listing 6-33. The SendGetImageDataCommand() function

```
void SendGetImageDataCommand()

{

        String Command = "GetImageData";


        // Set Up Data Handler

        m_WifiMessageHandler.ResetData();

        m_WifiMessageHandler.SetDataReceiveLength(m_PhotoSize);

        m_TakePhotoState = TakePhotoCallbackState.GetImageData;

        m_WifiMessageHandler.SetCommand(Command);

        if (m_ClientConnectThread != null)

        {

                if (m_ClientConnectThread.IsConnected())

                {

                        m_TakePhotoButton.setEnabled(false);

                        m_ClientConnectThread.write(Command.getBytes());
```

```
                    m_DebugMsg += "Writing GetImageData command to CC3200!! Command = " +
Command + "\n";

            }

        else

        {

                m_DebugMsg += "ConnectedThread is Null!! \n";

        }

    }

else

{

        m_DebugMsg += "ClientConnectThread is Null!! \n";

}

m_DebugMsgView.setText(m_DebugMsg.toCharArray(), 0, m_DebugMsg.length());

}
```

The MovementProcessing() Function

The MovementProcessing() function processes movement by

1. Detecting any movement present by calling the MovementDetected() function.

2. If movement is detected then determine if the alarm has been tripped and store the result in m_AlarmTripped.

3. Return a true value if motion is detected and false if no motion has been detected.

See Listing 6-34.

Listing 6-34. The MovementProcessing() function

```
boolean MovementProcessing()

{

        boolean result = false;

        if (MovementDetected())

        {

                m_AlarmTripped = TripAlarm();
```

```
                result = true;

        }

        return result;

}
```

The MovementDetected() Function

The MovementDetected() function determines if there is movement between two consecutive frames that are captured during surveillance by:

1. If the SAD value that was calculated between the current frame and the previous frame is greater than the SAD threshold value then motion has been detected.

2. If motion has been detected then assign the current value of SAD which is held in m_SAD to m_SADTripped.

3. If motion has been detected return a true value otherwise return a false value.

See Listing 6-35.

Listing 6-35. The MovementDetected() function

```
boolean MovementDetected()

{

        boolean result = false;


        m_SADThreshold = m_SADCalcThreshold;

        if (m_SAD > m_SADThreshold)

        {

                // Movement detected

                m_SADTripped = m_SAD;

                result = true;

        }

        return result;

}
```

The TripAlarm() Function

The TripAlarm() function trips the alarm if the required number of motions have been detected within a certain timeframe. This timeframe is called the false positive time interval and is used to screen out false positive motions caused by camera noise.

The TripAlarm() function does the following:

1. If the alarm is already tripped then there is no need to update the tripped status.

2. If this is the first time that motions have been detected then set the m_FalsePositiveStartTime variable to the result from the call to the System.currentTimeMillis() function which returns the current time in milliseconds. Set the m_FalsePositiveTestStarted variable to true to indicate that the false positive interval testing has started.

3. Retrieve the current time.

4. Calculate the elapsed time by finding the difference between the current time and the false positive testing start time.

5. If the elapsed time is less than or equal to m_FalsePositiveTimeInterval which is the false positive time interval set by the user then increase m_NumberMotionsDetected which is the number of motions detected.

6. If the elapsed time is greater then the false positive time interval then set the m_NumberMotionsDetected variable to 1. This resets the number of motions detected to just the current motion that was detected since the false positive time interval has passed without the required number of detected motions to trip the alarm. Set the m_FalsePositiveStartTime which is the starting time of the false positive interval to the current time. This resets the false positive time interval.

7. If the number of detected motions during the current false positive time interval is equal to or greater than the minimum number of motions needed for the alarm to trip then return a true result for the function otherwise return false.

See Listing 6-36.

Listing 6-36. The TripAlarm() function

```
boolean TripAlarm()

{

        boolean result = false;


        // Trip alarm if required number of motions have been detected within a

        // certain timeframe.
```

```
// If alarm already tripped then no need to update status

if (m_AlarmTripped)

{

        return true;

}


if (!m_FalsePositiveTestStarted)

{

        m_FalsePositiveStartTime = System.currentTimeMillis();

        m_FalsePositiveTestStarted = true;

}


m_CurTime = System.currentTimeMillis();

long Elapsed = m_CurTime - m_FalsePositiveStartTime;

if (Elapsed <= m_FalsePositiveTimeInterval)

{

        m_NumberMotionsDetected ++;

}

else

{

        // reset since too much time has passed between

        // detected motions

        m_NumberMotionsDetected = 1;

        m_FalsePositiveStartTime = System.currentTimeMillis();

}


if (m_NumberMotionsDetected >= m_MinimumMotionsForAlarmTrip)

{

        // Trip alarm
```

```
                result = true;

        }

        return result;

}
```

The CheckProcessCallout() Function

The CheckProcessCallout() function processes the emergency phone call out function once the alarm has been tripped by doing the following:

1. If the emergency phone call out has been set by the user and has not been done then call the emergency phone number by calling the CallEmergencyPhoneNumber() function. Set the m_CallOutDone variable to true.

2. If the emergency phone call out has not been set by the user and the emergency message has not been done then use the Android's text to speech function to notify the user that the alarm has been tripped. A sound effect that loops indefinitely is played. The m_EmergencyMessageDone variable is set to true;

See Listing 6-37.

Listing 6-37. The CheckProcessCallout() function

```
void CheckProcessCallout()

{

        // Check to see if callout is active and not yet done

        if (m_CallOutSet && !m_CallOutDone)

        {

                // Call emergency number and set call out done flag

                CallEmergencyPhoneNumber();

                m_CallOutDone = true;

        }

        else

        if (!m_CallOutSet && !m_EmergencyMessageDone)

        {

                // Repeat message

                for (int i = 0; i < m_EmergencyMessageRepeatTimes ; i++)
```

```
                    {

                        m_TTS.speak("Intruder Alert Intruder has been detected by the motion sensor",
TextToSpeech.QUEUE_ADD, null);

                    }


                m_Alert2SFX.PlaySound(true);

                m_EmergencyMessageDone = true;

        }

}
```

The CallEmergencyPhoneNumber() Function

The CallEmergencyPhoneNumber() function actually makes the call by the Android cell phone to the emergency phone number by:

1. Creating a string consisting of "tel:" and the emergency phone number without any trailing newline or other white space characters such as tab, space, etc.

2. Creating a new Intent class object which is set to call out to a phone number.

3. Setting the phone number in the intent object to the emergency phone number from Step 1 by calling the setData() function.

4. Dialing this phone number by calling the startActivity(intent) function with the intent from Step 2 as an input parameter.

See Listing 6-38.

Listing 6-38. The CallEmergencyPhoneNumber() function

```
void CallEmergencyPhoneNumber()

{

        // Call emergency number so that home owner can listen in to what tripped the

        // intruder alarm

        String uri = "tel:" + m_EmergencyPhoneNumber.trim();

        Intent intent = new Intent(Intent.ACTION_CALL);

        intent.setData(Uri.parse(uri));

        startActivity(intent);
```

}

The CheckProcessTextMessages() Function

The CheckProcessTextMessages() function processes the emergency text message alert function when the alarm has been tripped by doing the following:

1. If the emergency text message alert has already been sent then exit the function.

2. If the emergency text message alert has not been sent and the user has requested that a text message be sent then send the alert by calling the SendEmergencySMSText() function. Set the m_TextMessageSent variable to true.

See Listing 6-39.

Listing 6-39. The CheckProcessTextMessages() function

```
void CheckProcessTextMessages()

{

        if (m_TextMessageSent)

        {

                return;

        }


        if (m_TextMessagesSetting == TextMessageSetting.TEXT_ON)

        {

                SendEmergencySMSText();

                m_TextMessageSent = true;

        }

}
```

The SendEmergencySMSText() Function

The SendEmergencySMSText() function sends an SMS emergency text alert message by doing the following:

1. Creates the emergency text message and assigns it to the EmergencyMessage variable.

2. Sends an SMS text message by calling the SendSMS(EmergencyMessage) function with the text message created in step 1.

Note: The maximum number of characters for a text message is 160 characters and depending on the encoding for your particular cell phone network the number of available characters may be significantly less.

See Listing 6-40.

L:isting 6-40. The SendEmergencySMSText() Function

```
void SendEmergencySMSText()

{

        String EmergencyMessage = "***Intruder Detected, Number Motions Detected: " +
m_NumberMotionsDetected;

        SendSMS(EmergencyMessage);

}
```

The SendSMS() Function

The SendSMS() function does the actual job of sending an SMS text message to the emergency phone number.

The function does the following:

1. Retrieve a SmsManager object by calling the SmsManager.getDefault() function. The returned object is assigned to the TextMessageManager variable.

2. Sends the actual text message to the emergency phone number by calling the TextMessageManager.sendTextMessage(m_EmergencyPhoneNumber, null, Msg, null, null) function. The first parameter is the phone number to send the text message to. The third parameter is the actual text message that is sent. The rest of the parameters are not needed so they are set to null.

3. A message is displayed that contains the text "Emergency Text Message Sent to " and then the number held in the m_EmergencyPhoneNumber variable.

4. A message is displayed that contains the text message that was sent.

See Listing 6-41.

Listing 6-41. The SendSMS() function

```
void SendSMS(String Msg)

{

        SmsManager TextMessageManager = SmsManager.getDefault();
```

//TextMessageManager.sendTextMessage(destinationAddress, scAddress, text, sentIntent, deliveryIntent);

TextMessageManager.sendTextMessage(m_EmergencyPhoneNumber, null, Msg, null, null);

Toast.makeText(this, "Emergency Text Message Sent to " +
m_EmergencyPhoneNumber,Toast.LENGTH_LONG).show();

Toast.makeText(this, Msg,Toast.LENGTH_LONG).show();

}

The SavePicJPEG() Function

The SavePicJPEG() function saves the photo that was transmitted to the Android from the CC3200 by:

1. Creating the beginning of the filename from the image resolution such as VGA, QVGA or QQVGA.

2. Creating the date by first getting a Calendar class object by calling the Calendar.getInstance() function. Then using this object to get the month, day of the month, year, hour, minute, and second and adding this to the end of the filename.

3. Adding the ".jpg" extension to the filename.

4. Creating a new file using the filename in the directory specified by m_CameraDir.

5. Writing out the image data that is in the m_PhotoData array to the file.

6. If surveillance is active then assign the filename created to the m_SurveillanceFileName String variable.

See Listing 6-42.

Listing 6-42. The SavePicJPEG() funciton

```
String SavePicJPEG()

{

        // Main Filename

        String Filename = m_Resolution.toString() + "_";


        // Add Date

        Calendar rightNow = Calendar.getInstance();

        int Month          =          rightNow.get(Calendar.MONTH);
```

```
int DayOfMonth     =          rightNow.get(Calendar.DAY_OF_MONTH);

int Year           =          rightNow.get(Calendar.YEAR);

int Hour           =          rightNow.get(Calendar.HOUR_OF_DAY);

int Minute         =          rightNow.get(Calendar.MINUTE);

int Second         =          rightNow.get(Calendar.SECOND);


String Date = Month + "_" + DayOfMonth + "_" + Year + "_" + Hour + "_" + Minute + "_" + Second;


// Add JPG Extension

String Extension = ".jpg";


// Build Final Filename

Filename += Date;

Filename += Extension;


// Open File to write out image data

File file = new File(m_CameraDir, Filename);

try

{

        OutputStream os = new FileOutputStream(file);

        os.write(m_PhotoData, 0, m_PhotoSize);

        os.close();

}

catch (IOException e)

{

        // Unable to create file, likely because external storage is

        // not currently mounted.

        Log.e("ExternalStorage", "Error writing " + file, e);

        AddDebugMessage(TAG + ": Error writing " + file);
```

```
        }


        // If surveillance is active then record the filename that the photo was saved to.

        if (m_SurveillanceActive)

        {

                m_SurveillanceFileName = Filename;

        }

        return Filename;

}
```

The CalculateSADThresHold() Function

The CalculateSADThresHold() function calculates the SAD threshold that is used to determine if there is enough differences in the pixels between image frames that motion has been detected.

The function does the following:

1. If the number of SAD calibration iterations is equal to or greater than the required number of iterations then calculate the SAD threshold. The SAD threshold is calculated as the sum of the highest SAD value calculated in the calibration phase added to a percentage of that value. The percentage is the threshold percent error and is determined by user menu selections. In code it is: m_SADCalcThreshold = (int)(m_SADHighest + (m_SADThresholdPercentError * m_SADHighest));

2. If the number of SAD calibrations is less than the required number of SAD calibrations then increase the SAD counter for calibration. If the current SAD value is greater than the highest SAD calibration value then set the highest SAD calibration value to the current SAD value.

See Listing 6-43.

Listing 6-43. The CalculateSADThresHold() function

```
void CalculateSADThresHold()

{

        if (m_SADCount >= m_SADCalcNumIterations)

        {

                m_SADCalcThreshold = (int)(m_SADHighest + (m_SADThresholdPercentError *
m_SADHighest));

                m_SADCalibrationDone = true;
```

```
        }

        else

        {

                // Find highest level of SAD

                if (m_SAD > m_SADHighest)

                {

                        m_SADHighest = m_SAD;

                }

                m_SADCount++;

                m_SADCalibrationDone = false;

        }

}
```

The SendTakePhotoCommand() Function

The SendTakePhotoCommand() function starts a Take Photo command by:

1. Setting the command to send to the CC3200 to the current user selected resolution such as VGA, QVGA, or QQVGA.

2. Resets the data in the wifi message handler by calling the m_WifiMessageHandler.ResetData() function.

3. Sets the command in the message handler to one that matches the type of return value expected from the CC3200 which is the GetImageSize command. The data type expected is the size of the photo in bytes that was just taken by the camera.

4. The state of the Take Photo command is set to the GetImageSize state.

5. The Take Photo button is disabled.

6. The command created in Step 1 is converted from a String object into an array of bytes and transmitted to the CC3200.

See Figure 6-44.

Listing 6-44. The SendTakePhotoCommand() function

```
void SendTakePhotoCommand()

{
```

```
String Command = m_Resolution.toString();


// Set Up Data Handler

m_WifiMessageHandler.ResetData();

m_WifiMessageHandler.SetCommand("GetImageSize");

m_TakePhotoState = TakePhotoCallbackState.GetImageSize;

if (m_ClientConnectThread != null)

{

        if (m_ClientConnectThread.IsConnected())

        {

                m_TakePhotoButton.setEnabled(false);

                m_ClientConnectThread.write(Command.getBytes());

                m_DebugMsg += "Writing Take Photo Command Message to Arduino!! \n";

        }

        else

        {

                m_DebugMsg += "ConnectedThread is Null!! \n";

        }

}

else

{

        m_DebugMsg += "ClientConnectThread is Null!! \n";

}

m_DebugMsgView.setText(m_DebugMsg.toCharArray(), 0, m_DebugMsg.length());

}
```

The AddDebugMessage() Function

The AddDebugMessage() function adds a String text message to the current debug message and updates the debug message window to reflect the change. See Listing 6-45.

Listing 6-45. The AddDebugMessage() function

```
public void AddDebugMessage(String Message)

{

        m_DebugMsg += Message;

        m_DebugMsgView.setText(m_DebugMsg.toCharArray(), 0, m_DebugMsg.length());

}
```

The AddDebugMessageThread() Function

The AddDebugMessageThread() function is called from another thread such as the Client class and adds a text string to the existing debug message. It also sets the debug message window to refresh when the run() function is executed by setting the m_RefreshMessageWindows to true. See Listing 6-46.

Listing 6-46. The AddDebugMessageThread() function

```
public void AddDebugMessageThread(String Message)

{

        m_DebugMsg += Message;

        m_RefreshMessageWindows = true;

}
```

The WifiSocketConnectedMessage() Function

The WifiSocketConnectedMessage() function is called from the Client class when a wifi connection has been established with the CC3200 device. The function notifies the user that the wifi connection is now active, sets the "take photo" button to active, and sets up the debug and output message windows to be updated when the run() function is called. See Listing 6-47.

Listing 6-47. The WifiSocketConnectedMessage() function

```
void WifiSocketConnectedMessage()

{

        m_TTS.speak("Wifi Socket Is now Connected", TextToSpeech.QUEUE_ADD, null);

        Log.e(TAG , "WIfi Socket is Now Connected ...");
```

m_DebugMsg += "Wifi Socket Is Now Connected ...\n";

// Activate Take Photo Button

m_TakePhotoButtonActive = true;

// Refresh Message Windows

m_RefreshMessageWindows = true;

}

The TakePhotoCommandCallback() Function

The TakePhotoCommandCallback() function is called from the WifiMessageHandler class after a request for information either the image size or the image data regarding a "take photo" command has been completed and the data is ready to be processed. If it is the image data then the m_PhotoData variable is set to point to the binary image data. The m_TakePhotoCallbackDone variable is set to true so that the incoming data will be processed in the run() command.

See Listing 6-47.

Listing 6-47. The TakePhotoCommandCallback() function

void TakePhotoCommandCallback()

{

        // Photo is now ready for viewing

        m_TakePhotoCallbackDone = true;

        if (m_TakePhotoState == TakePhotoCallbackState.GetImageData)

        {

                m_PhotoData = m_WifiMessageHandler.GetBinaryData();

        }

}

The onDestroy() Function

The onDestroy() function is called when the application is being terminated and does the following:

1. Stops the playing of any sound effects that may be active by calling the StopSounds() function.

2. Shuts down the Android text to speech function by calling the m_TTS.shutdown() function.

3. If there is a wifi connection between the Android and the CC3200 then send a terminate server command to the CC3200 by calling the SendTerminateServerCommand() function. Cancel the wifi connection by calling the m_ClientConnectThread.cancel() function.

4. If there is not a wifi connection between the Android and the CC3200 then stop the execution of the Client class by calling the m_ClientConnectThread.Freeze() function.

5. Turn off the Android wifi by calling the m_ClientConnectThread.m_WifiManager.setWifiEnabled(false) function with false as the input parameter.

6. Discard the Client thread so that there are no more references to the Client object and it can be erased from the Android's memory by the memory manager by setting the m_ClientConnectThread to null.

See Listing 6-48.

Listing 6-48. The onDestroy() function

```
@Override

protected void onDestroy()

{

        Log.e(TAG, "In onDestroy() FUNCTION !!!!!!!!");

        super.onDestroy();


        // Stop playing sound effects

        StopSounds();


        // Shutdown Text To Speech

        m_TTS.shutdown();


        // Shutdown Client Thread to Server

        if (m_ClientConnectThread != null)

        {
```

```
            if (m_ClientConnectThread.IsConnected())

            {

                    // Terminate TDP Server running on CC3200

                    SendTerminateServerCommand();


                    // Close Client Thread

                    Log.e(TAG, "Cancelling Client Connect Thread!!!!!!!!");

                    m_ClientConnectThread.cancel();

            }
            else

            {

                    // Thread not connected to server so freeze its execution

                    m_ClientConnectThread.Freeze();

            }

    }


    // Turn off Wifi

    m_ClientConnectThread.m_WifiManager.setWifiEnabled(false);


    // Discard Thread

    m_ClientConnectThread = null;

}
```

The SendTerminateServerCommand() Function

The SendTerminateServerCommand() function sends a "terminate" command string to the CC3200 device which terminates and then restarts the TCP server that is running on the CC3200. See Listing 6-49.

Listing 6-49. The SendTerminateServerCommand() function

```
void SendTerminateServerCommand()
```

```
{

        String Command = "terminate";


        // Set Up Data Handler

        m_WifiMessageHandler.ResetData();

        m_WifiMessageHandler.SetCommand("terminate");

        if (m_ClientConnectThread != null)

        {

                if (m_ClientConnectThread.IsConnected())

                {

                        m_TakePhotoButton.setEnabled(false);

                        m_ClientConnectThread.write(Command.getBytes());

                        Log.e(TAG, "Sending terminate command to TCP Server ...");

                }

        }

}
```

The Android Manifest File

The Android manifest file is an xml file that holds key information such as permissions and minimum operating system requirements. The permissions in the following code are highlighted in bold. The other important item is the line:

android:windowSoftInputMode="adjustPan"

which sets the Android virtual keyboard so that when the keyboard is displayed a portion of the screen is scrolled upward so that the emergency phone text entry box is visible.

See Listing 6-50.

Listing 6-50. The Android Manifest file

```
<?xml version="1.0" encoding="utf-8"?>

<manifest xmlns:android="http://schemas.android.com/apk/res/android"

  package="com.example.gotchacam"
```

```
android:versionCode="1"

android:versionName="1.0" >


<uses-sdk

    android:minSdkVersion="8"

    android:targetSdkVersion="16" />
<uses-permission android:name="android.permission.ACCESS_WIFI_STATE"/>

<uses-permission android:name="android.permission.CHANGE_WIFI_STATE"/>

<uses-permission android:name="android.permission.ACCESS_NETWORK_STATE"/>

<uses-permission android:name="android.permission.CHANGE_NETWORK_STATE"/>

<uses-permission android:name="android.permission.INTERNET"/>

<uses-permission android:name="android.permission.WAKE_LOCK"/>

<uses-permission android:name="android.permission.WRITE_EXTERNAL_STORAGE"/>

<uses-permission android:name="android.permission.CALL_PHONE"/>

<uses-permission android:name="android.permission.SEND_SMS"/>


<application

    android:allowBackup="true"

    android:icon="@drawable/ic_launcher"

    android:label="@string/app_name"

    android:theme="@style/AppTheme" >

    <activity

        android:name="com.example.gotchacam.MainActivity"


        android:windowSoftInputMode="adjustPan"


        android:label="@string/app_name" >

        <intent-filter>

            <action android:name="android.intent.action.MAIN" />
```

```
            <category android:name="android.intent.category.LAUNCHER" />

        </intent-filter>

    </activity>

  </application>

</manifest>
```

The Graphic User Interface Code

The graphic user interface xml code is in the res/layout directory and is shown in Listing 6-51. The code highlighted in bold are the resource ids that are used to identify the user interface items in the MainActivity class code.

Listing 6-51. The application graphical user interface code

```
<RelativeLayout xmlns:android="http://schemas.android.com/apk/res/android"

  xmlns:tools="http://schemas.android.com/tools"

  android:layout_width="match_parent"

  android:layout_height="match_parent"

  tools:context=".MainActivity" >


  <ImageView

    android:id="@+id/imageView1"

    android:layout_width="320dp"

    android:layout_height="240dp"

    android:layout_alignParentLeft="true"

    android:layout_alignParentTop="true"

    android:src="@drawable/ic_launcher" />


  <Button

    android:id="@+id/TestMessageButton"

    android:layout_width="wrap_content"

    android:layout_height="wrap_content"
```

```
        android:layout_alignParentRight="true"

        android:layout_alignTop="@+id/phoneentry"

        android:text="Take Photo" />


    <EditText

        android:id="@+id/phoneentry"

        android:layout_width="wrap_content"

        android:layout_height="wrap_content"

        android:layout_alignParentLeft="true"

        android:layout_below="@+id/imageView1"

        android:layout_toLeftOf="@+id/TestMessageButton"

        android:ems="10"

        android:lines="3"

        android:maxLines="3"

        android:inputType="phone" />


    <EditText

        android:id="@+id/debugmsg"

        android:layout_width="wrap_content"

        android:layout_height="wrap_content"

        android:layout_alignParentLeft="true"

        android:layout_alignRight="@+id/phoneentry"

        android:layout_below="@+id/phoneentry"

        android:ems="10"

        android:lines="6"

        android:maxLines="6"

        />


    <EditText
```

```
    android:id="@+id/textView1"

    android:layout_width="wrap_content"

    android:layout_height="wrap_content"

    android:layout_alignLeft="@+id/TestMessageButton"

    android:layout_alignParentRight="true"

    android:layout_alignTop="@+id/debugmsg"

    android:ems="10"

    android:scrollHorizontally="true"

    android:scrollbarStyle="outsideOverlay"

    android:scrollbars="vertical"

    android:text="TextView"

    android:textSize="11dp" >


    <requestFocus />

  </EditText>


</RelativeLayout>
```

The Menu Settings Code

The code for the menu items for the application is located in the res/menu directory and is shown in Listing 6-52.

Listing 6-52. The menu settings code

```
<menu xmlns:android="http://schemas.android.com/apk/res/android" >

  <item

    android:id="@+id/callout_settings"

    android:orderInCategory="100"

    android:showAsAction="never"

    android:title="Call Out Settings">

    <menu>
```

```
                <item android:id="@+id/callout_on" android:title="Turn On Emergency Call Out"/>

                <item android:id="@+id/callout_off" android:title="Turn Off Emergency Call Out"/>

            </menu>

        </item>

        <item android:id="@+id/alarm_settings" android:title="Alarm Settings">

            <menu>

                <item android:id="@+id/alarm_activate" android:title="Activate Alarm"/>

                <item android:id="@+id/alarm_deactivate" android:title="Deactivate Alarm"/>

            </menu>

        </item>

        <item android:id="@+id/textmess_settings" android:title="Text Message Settings">

            <menu>

                <item android:id="@+id/notext" android:title="No Text Messages" /><item android:id="@+id/text_only"
android:title="Text Messages On"/>

            </menu>

        </item>

        <item android:id="@+id/resolution_settings" android:title="Resolution Settings">

            <menu>

                <item android:id="@+id/qqvga" android:title="QQVGA (160 x 120)"/><item android:id="@+id/qvga"
android:title="QVGA (320 x 240)" /><item android:id="@+id/vga" android:title="VGA (640 x 480)"/>

            </menu>

        </item>

        <item android:id="@+id/surveillance" android:title="Surveillance Settings">

            <menu>

                <item android:id="@+id/surveillance_on" android:title="Turn On Surveillance"/>

                <item android:id="@+id/surveillance_off" android:title="Turn Off Surveillance"/>

            </menu>

        </item>

        <item android:id="@+id/loadandroidimage" android:title="Load Stored Image">

            <menu></menu>
```

```
    </item>

    <item android:id="@+id/androidstoragesettings" android:title="Android Storage Settings">

        <menu>

            <item android:id="@+id/androidstorageyes" android:title="Save Incoming Images"/>

            <item android:id="@+id/androidstorageno" android:title="Do NOT Save Incoming Images"/>

        </menu>

    </item>

    <item android:id="@+id/motiondetectaccuracy" android:title="Motion Detection Accuracy">

        <menu>

            <item android:id="@+id/motionhigh" android:title="High Accuracy"/>

            <item android:id="@+id/motionmedium" android:title="Medium Accuracy"/>

            <item android:id="@+id/motionlow" android:title="Lower Accuracy"/>

        </menu>

    </item>

    <item android:id="@+id/motiondetecttolerance" android:title="Motion Detection Tolerance">

        <menu>

            <item android:id="@+id/fivepercent" android:title="5% Tolerance"/>

            <item android:id="@+id/tenpercent" android:title="10% Tolerance"/>

            <item android:id="@+id/fifteenpercent" android:title="15% Tolerance"/>

            <item android:id="@+id/twentypercent" android:title="20% Tolerance"/>

            <item android:id="@+id/twentyfivepercent" android:title="25% Tolerance"/>

        </menu>

    </item>

    <item android:id="@+id/minimummotions" android:title="Minimum Motions for Alarm Trip">

        <menu>

            <item android:id="@+id/one" android:title="1 Motion"/>

            <item android:id="@+id/threemotions" android:title="3 Motions"/>

            <item android:id="@+id/fivemotions" android:title="5 Motions"/>

            <item android:id="@+id/eightmotions" android:title="8 Motions"/>
```

```
            <item android:id="@+id/elevenmotions" android:title="11 Motions"/>

        </menu>

    </item>

    <item android:id="@+id/falsepositive" android:title="False Positive Time Interval">

        <menu>

            <item android:id="@+id/fiveseconds" android:title="5 Seconds"/>

            <item android:id="@+id/tenseconds" android:title="10 Seconds"/>

            <item android:id="@+id/fifteenseconds" android:title="15 Seconds"/>

            <item android:id="@+id/twentyseconds" android:title="20 Seconds"/>

            <item android:id="@+id/twentyfive" android:title="25 Seconds"/>

        </menu>

    </item>

</menu>
```

Summary

In this chapter I covered the design and code implementation for the Android portion of the home security and surveillance system presented in this book. I started by giving an overview of how the entire security system worked including how the Android and the CC3200 devices interacted with each other. I then discussed how sound effects are handled on the Android device. Finally, I discussed how the alarm system logic, motion detection, user interface, and cell phone communication features are implemented in code inside the MainActivity class.

Chapter 7

The CC3200 Simplelink Wireless Security System Design

In this chapter I cover the design of the CC3200 Simplelink portion of the home security system presented in this book. I start by giving an overview of the key functional components of the CC3200 device and the associated source code that controls each of these components. Next I discuss the key CC3200 source code relating to the operation of the camera including the TCP server which processes the incoming commands from the Android device and sends out image related data. I then give an overview of the CC3200's direct memory access system or micro-DMA. I then discuss the camera interface followed by the camera related source code.

Design Overview

The CC3200 portion of the security system described in this book consists of:

1. A MT9D111 camera

2. A TI camera booster pack (If you are using a TI CC3200 Launchpad)

3. A TI CC3200 Launchpad or ArduCAM CC3200 Uno.

The key items from this system that will be discussed in this chapter are:

1. The MT9D111 camera

2. The DMA (direct memory access) transfer of the image data from the camera to the CC3200's main memory.

3. The camera interface configuration needed to successfully connect the camera to the CC3200 device for data transfer.

4. The memory configuration that allows the direct allocation of the CC3200 device's memory needed to get the security system to work

See Figure 7-1.

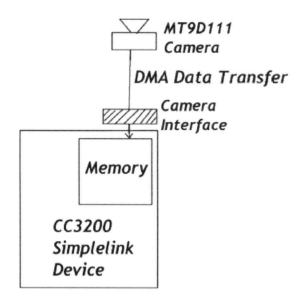

Figure 7-1. General Overview of the CC3200 System

The source code files associated with the key items are shown in Figure 7-2.

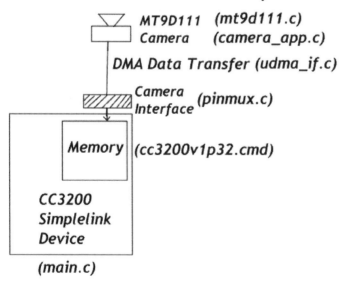

Figure 7-2. General Overview of Files

TI Code Composer Studio

The TI Code Composer Studio is based on the Eclipse IDE which is the same IDE as the Android ADT Bundle discussed in Chapter 3. The home security system project files are stored in the wlan_ap folder of the downloadable CC3200 source code I created. The CC3200 code for this project was built on top of the wlan_ap SDK example. See Chapter 8 for a listing of the downloadable files for this book. The key files are circled. The Release directory holds the final wlan_ap.bin executable file that is the file that needs to be written to the CC3200 device using Uniflash. See Figure 7-3.

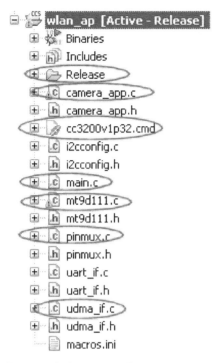

Figure 7-3. The project files

The Main Program Code

The code on the CC3200 side of this security system was built on top of the wlan_ap example from the TI CC3200 SDK. The wlan_ap example gives a good starting point for using the CC3200 as an access point. The key additions I made to the code were relating to using a TCP server to read in commands from the Android device and reply to these commands over a wifi connection.

The main() function is the starting point for the code execution on the CC3200 and it does the following:

1. The CC3200 device is initialized by calling the BoardInit() function.

2. Enable and configure the DMA (direct memory access) by calling the UDMAInit() function.

3. Configure the pinmux settings for the camera interface by calling the PinMuxConfig() function.

4. Configure the UART which allows for text debugging using a program such as TerraTerm by calling the InitTerm() function.

5. Output text to the UART that displays a banner indicating the program name by calling the DisplayBanner(APP_NAME) function with the string text "Robs WLAN AP".

6. Start the SimpleLink host by calling the VStartSimpleLinkSpawnTask(SPAWN_TASK_PRIORITY) function with spawn task priority of 9. An error value is returned and assigned to the lRetVal variable.

7. If the lRetVal is less than 0 then print out an error message and halt execution of the program.

8. Start the WlanAPMode() task by calling the osi_TaskCreate(WlanAPMode, (const signed char*)"wireless LAN in AP mode", OSI_STACK_SIZE, NULL, 1, NULL) function. The first parameter is the pointer to the task function that will be executed. The second parameter is the task name string. The third parameter is the size of the stack in 32-bit long words. The fourth parameter is the pointer to structure to be passed to the task function. The fifth parameter is the task priority. The last parameter is the task handle. The return value from the function is assigned to lRetVal.

9. If the lRetVal variable is less than 0 then print out an error message and halt execution of the program.

10. Start the task scheduler by calling the osi_start() function.

See Listing 7-1.

Listing 7-1. The main() function

```
void main()

{

        long lRetVal = -1;


        //

        // Board Initialization

        //

        BoardInit();


        //

        // Enable and configure DMA

        //

        UDMAInit();


        //

        // Configure the pinmux settings for the peripherals exercised

        //

        PinMuxConfig();
```

```
#ifndef NOTERM
            //
            // Configuring UART
            //
            InitTerm();
#endif


//
// Display banner
//
DisplayBanner(APP_NAME);


//
// Start the SimpleLink Host
//
lRetVal = VStartSimpleLinkSpawnTask(SPAWN_TASK_PRIORITY);
if(lRetVal < 0)
{
        ERR_PRINT(lRetVal);
        LOOP_FOREVER();
}


//
// Start the WlanAPMode task
//
lRetVal = osi_TaskCreate( WlanAPMode, \
        (const signed char*)"wireless LAN in AP mode", \
        OSI_STACK_SIZE, NULL, 1, NULL );
```

```
        if(lRetVal < 0)

        {

                ERR_PRINT(lRetVal);

                LOOP_FOREVER();

        }


        //

        // Start the task scheduler

        //

        osi_start();

}
```

The WlanAPMode() Function

The WlanAPMode() function creates the access point and the TCP server on the CC3200 by doing the following:

1. Key variables are initialized in this program by calling the InitializeAppVariables() function.

2. The CC3200 device is set to its initial factory state by clearing any settings such as connection profiles, power policy, etc and the device is put into station mode by calling the ConfigureSimpleLinkToDefaultState() function. The return value from the function call is assigned to the lRetVal variable. Refer to Chapter 4 for more information on this function.

3. If lRetVal is less than 0 then print out an error message and halt the execution of the program.

4. Start the Simplelink device which starts up the CC3200's wifi and networking capabilities by calling the sl_Start(NULL,NULL,NULL) function and assigning the returned value to the lRetVal variable.

5. if the lRetVal is less than 0 then print out an error message and halt the execution of the program.

6. The CC3200 is set to a access point mode by calling the ConfigureMode(lRetVal) function. If the CC3200 cannot be set into access point mode then shut down the Simplelink processor and halt program execution. For a detailed discussion of the ConfigureMode() function see Chapter 4.

7. Set the ip address of the CC3200 to a static ip address that does not change by calling the SetStaticIP() function. For a more detailed discussion of this function see Chapter 4.

8. Wait until the CC3200 acquires an ip address before continuing program execution.

9. Retrieve the network configuration by calling the sl_NetCfgGet(SL_IPV4_AP_P2P_GO_GET_INFO,&ucDHCP,&len, (unsigned char *)&ipV4) function. The return error code is assigned to the lRetVal variable.

10. Print out the network configuration info that was retrieved in step 9 and put into the ipV4 variable by calling the PrintIPInfo(ipV4) function with the ipV4 variable as the parameter.

11. Wait for a client (the Android device) to connect to the CC3200 device before continuing program execution.

12. Creates the TCP server that will be handling the communication with the Android client device by calling the BsdTcpServer(PORT_NUM) function with the port number that the server is to be listening to for a connection request.

13. If the server is terminated by a command from the Android device then go to step 12 to restart the server

See Listing 7-2.

Listing 7-2. The WlanAPMode() function

```
void WlanAPMode( void *pvParameters )

{

    int iTestResult = 0;

    unsigned char ucDHCP;

    long lRetVal = -1;


    InitializeAppVariables();


    //

    // Following function configure the device to default state by cleaning

    // the persistent settings stored in NVMEM (viz. connection profiles &

    // policies, power policy etc)

    //

    // Applications may choose to skip this step if the developer is sure

    // that the device is in its default state at start of applicaton

    //

    // Note that all profiles and persistent settings that were done on the
```

```
// device will be lost

//

lRetVal = ConfigureSimpleLinkToDefaultState();

if(lRetVal < 0)

{

    if (DEVICE_NOT_IN_STATION_MODE == lRetVal)

        UART_PRINT("Failed to configure the device in its default state \n\r");


        LOOP_FOREVER();

}


UART_PRINT("Device is configured in default state \n\r");


//

// Asumption is that the device is configured in station mode already

// and it is in its default state

//

lRetVal = sl_Start(NULL,NULL,NULL);


if (lRetVal < 0)

{

    UART_PRINT("Failed to start the device \n\r");

    LOOP_FOREVER();

}


UART_PRINT("Device started as STATION \n\r");


//

// Configure the networking mode and ssid name(for AP mode)
```

212

```
//

if(lRetVal != ROLE_AP)

{

    if(ConfigureMode(lRetVal) != ROLE_AP)

    {

        UART_PRINT("Unable to set AP mode, exiting Application...\n\r");

        sl_Stop(SL_STOP_TIMEOUT);

        LOOP_FOREVER();

    }

}


// Set CC3200 in AP mode with a Static IP Address

SetStaticIP();


while(!IS_IP_ACQUIRED(g_ulStatus))

{

  //looping till ip is acquired

}


unsigned char len = sizeof(SlNetCfgIpV4Args_t);

SlNetCfgIpV4Args_t ipV4 = {0};


// get network configuration

lRetVal = sl_NetCfgGet(SL_IPV4_AP_P2P_GO_GET_INFO,&ucDHCP,&len,

                (unsigned char *)&ipV4);


// Print out Network Configuration Info

PrintIPInfo(ipV4);
```

```
if (lRetVal < 0)

{

    UART_PRINT("Failed to get network configuration \n\r");

    LOOP_FOREVER();

}


UART_PRINT("Connect a client to Device ...\n\r");

while(!IS_IP_LEASED(g_ulStatus))

{

    //wating for the client to connect

}

UART_PRINT("Client is connected to Device ...\n\r");


UNUSED(ucDHCP);

UNUSED(iTestResult);


// TCP Server Loop

// Start TCP Server. If application terminates then terminate current TCP

// Server and start brand new TCP Server and wait for new connection.

while (1)

{

        UART_PRINT("Starting TCP Server ...\n\r");

        lRetVal = BsdTcpServer(PORT_NUM);

        if (lRetVal < 0)

        {

                UART_PRINT("TCP Server Creation Failed !!!\n\r");

        }

        else

        {
```

```
                    UART_PRINT("TCP Server Creation Succeeded !!!\n\r");

        }

    }

}
```

The BsdTcpServer() Function

The BsdTcpServer() function creates and manages the server for communication with the Android client device over a wifi connection. I discuss this function fully in Chapter 4. The code in Listing 7-3 that is shown in bold print is the key code that handles communication with the Android client device.

Listing 7-3. The BsdTcpServer() function

```
static int BsdTcpServer(unsigned short Port)

{

        SlSockAddrIn_t  Addr;

        SlSockAddrIn_t  LocalAddr;


        int       idx;

        int       AddrSize;

        int       SockID;

        int       Status;

        int       newSockID;

        long       LoopCount = 0;

        long       nonBlocking = 1;

        int                              done = -1;


        for (idx=0 ; idx<BUF_SIZE ; idx++)

        {

                uBuf.BsdBuf[idx] = (char)(idx % 10);

        }
```

```
LocalAddr.sin_family = SL_AF_INET;

LocalAddr.sin_port = sl_Htons((unsigned short)Port);

LocalAddr.sin_addr.s_addr = 0;


SockID = sl_Socket(SL_AF_INET,SL_SOCK_STREAM, 0);

ASSERT_ON_ERROR(SockID);

if (SockID < 0)

{

        Report("sl_Socket() function FAILED !!!\n\r");

}

else

{

        Report("sl_Socket() operation ok ...\n\r");

}


AddrSize = sizeof(SlSockAddrIn_t);

Status = sl_Bind(SockID, (SlSockAddr_t *)&LocalAddr, AddrSize);

if( Status < 0 )

{

        /* error */

        sl_Close(SockID);

        ASSERT_ON_ERROR(Status);

}

else

{

        Report("sl_Bind operation ok ...\n\r");

}
```

```
Status = sl_Listen(SockID, 0);

if( Status < 0 )

{

        sl_Close(SockID);

        ASSERT_ON_ERROR(Status);

}

else

{

        Report("sl_Listen() operation ok ...\n\r");

}


Status = sl_SetSockOpt(SockID, SL_SOL_SOCKET, SL_SO_NONBLOCKING,

        &nonBlocking, sizeof(nonBlocking));

ASSERT_ON_ERROR(Status);

if (Status < 0)

{

        Report("sl_SetSockOpt operation FAILED !!!\n\r");

}

else

{

        Report("sl_SetSockOpt operation ok ... \n\r");

}


Report ("Waiting for sl_Accept operation to complete ... \n\r");

newSockID = SL_EAGAIN;


while( newSockID < 0 &&  IS_IP_ACQUIRED(g_ulStatus))

{

        newSockID = sl_Accept(SockID, ( struct SlSockAddr_t *)&Addr,
```

```
                              (SlSocklen_t*)&AddrSize);

            if( newSockID == SL_EAGAIN )

            {

                        /* Wait for 1 ms */

                        Delay(1);

            }

            else if( newSockID < 0 )

            {

                        sl_Close(SockID);

                        ASSERT_ON_ERROR(newSockID);

                        Report ("sl_Accept Error - Socket ID < 0 ...\n\r");

            }

            else

            {

                        // Operation Finished

                        Report("sl_Accept operation ok ...\n\r");

            }

}


Report("Finished Accept ...\n\r");

if(! IS_IP_ACQUIRED(g_ulStatus))

{

            return -1;

}


Report ("Ready to recieve data using sl_Recv\n\r");


// Initialize Camera to QVGA resolution

int width = 320;
```

```
int height = 240;

if (g_CameraInit == 0)

{

        InitializeCamera(width, height);

        g_CameraInit = 1;

}


while (done <= 0)

{

        Status = sl_Recv(newSockID, uBuf.BsdBuf, BUF_SIZE, 0);

        if (Status > 0)

        {

                // Process incoming data

                // Put terminating character at end of raw data to make it a valid string

                uBuf.BsdBuf[Status] = '\0';


                // Check if Need to Terminate Server

                if (strcmp(uBuf.BsdBuf, "terminate") == 0)

                {

                        Report("******* Terminate TCP Server Command Issued by Android
Client\n\r");

                        done = 1;

                }

                else

                if (strcmp(uBuf.BsdBuf, "VGA") == 0)

                {

                        // Change resolution if needed

                        if (g_CameraResolution != VGA)

                        {

                                // Set VGA Mode
```

```
                              SetCameraResolution(640, 480);

                              g_CameraResolution = VGA;

                    }


                    // Take Picture and return the size of the image taken

                    g_ImageSize = CameraCaptureImage();


                    // Send picture size to Android

                    TransmitCapturedImageSize(newSockID);

          }

          else

          if (strcmp(uBuf.BsdBuf, "QVGA") == 0)

          {

                    // Change resolution if needed

                    if (g_CameraResolution != QVGA)

                    {

                              // Set QVGA Mode

                              SetCameraResolution(320, 240);

                              g_CameraResolution = QVGA;

                    }


                    // Take Picture and return the size of the image taken

                    g_ImageSize = CameraCaptureImage();


                    // Send picture size to Android

                    TransmitCapturedImageSize(newSockID);

          }

          else

          if (strcmp(uBuf.BsdBuf, "QQVGA") == 0)
```

```
                    {
                            // Change resolution if needed

                            if (g_CameraResolution != QQVGA)

                            {
                                    // Set QVGA Mode

                                    SetCameraResolution(160, 120);

                                    g_CameraResolution = QQVGA;

                            }


                            // Take Picture and return the size of the image taken

                            g_ImageSize = CameraCaptureImage();


                            // Send picture size to Android

                            TransmitCapturedImageSize(newSockID);

                    }
                    else

                    if (strcmp(uBuf.BsdBuf, "GetImageData") == 0)

                    {
                            // Send Image Data for Camera

                            TransmitCapturedImage(newSockID);

                    }
            }
            else

            if( Status <= 0 )

            {
                    /* error */

                    ASSERT_ON_ERROR(sl_Close(newSockID));

                    ASSERT_ON_ERROR(sl_Close(SockID));

                    ASSERT_ON_ERROR(Status);
```

```
                    Report("ERROR reading data using sl_Recv() fuction ... \n\r");

            }

        }


        Report ("Finished recieving data ...\n\r");


        ASSERT_ON_ERROR(sl_Close(newSockID));

        ASSERT_ON_ERROR(sl_Close(SockID));


        return SUCCESS;

}
```

The InitializeCamera() Function

The InitializeCamera() function initializes the MT9D111 camera for use with the CC3200 device by calling the InitCameraComponents(width, height) function with the image capture width and height in pixels. See Listing 7-4.

Listing 7-4. The InitCameraComponents() function

```
void InitializeCamera(int width, int height)

{

        InitCameraComponents(width, height);

}
```


The CameraCaptureImage() Function

The CameraCaptureImage() function captures an image from the MT9D111 camera that is attached to the CC3200 through the camera port by calling the StartCamera((char **)&g_pCameraData) function with the g_pCameraData variable that is a pointer to a pointer that is used to retrieve the camera image data after it is captured. The size of the captured image in bytes is returned. See Listing 7-5.

Listing 7-5. The CameraCaptureImage function()

```
unsigned short CameraCaptureImage()

{

        unsigned short uLength = 0;

        uLength = StartCamera((char **)&g_pCameraData);

        return uLength;

}
```

The TransmitCapturedImageSize() Function

The TransmitCapturedImageSize() sends the size of the captured image to the Android client over the wifi connection by calling the sl_Send(SocketID, temp, strlen(temp), 0) function. The first parameter is the socket id to send the data through. The second parameter is an array of characters terminated by a newline character that is the size of the image. The third parameter is the length of the temp array. The final parameter is not supported for TCP and is set to 0.

See Listing 7-6.

Listing 7-6. The TransmitCapturedImageSize() function

```
int TransmitCapturedImageSize(int SocketID)

{

        char temp[50];

        int Status = -1;


        // Send File Length to Android Client

        sprintf(temp, "%d\n", g_ImageSize);

        Status = sl_Send(SocketID, temp, strlen(temp), 0);

        if (Status < 0)

        {

                Report("ERROR! sl_Send() command failed !!!\n\r");

        }


        return Status;
```

}

The TransmitCapturedImage() Function

The TransmitCapturedImage() function sends the image data from the CC3200 device to the Android device over the wifi connection by calling the sl_Send(SocketID, g_pCameraData, g_ImageSize, 0) function. The first parameter is the socket id to send the data through. The second parameter is the camera image data that was just captured. The third parameter is the size of the image that was just captured. The last parameter is not used for TCP and is set to 0.

See Listing 7-7.

Listing 7-7. The TransmitCapturedImage() function

```
int TransmitCapturedImage(int SocketID)

{

        int Status = -1;


        // Send Data to Android cient using WiFi

        Status = sl_Send(SocketID, g_pCameraData, g_ImageSize, 0);

        if (Status < 0)

        {

                Report("ERROR! sl_Send() command failed !!!\n\r");

        }

        return Status;

}
```

CC3200 Micro-DMA Overview

The CC3200 has a DMA or direct memory transfer system called micro-DMA. What DMA or direct memory access does is provide a way for devices such as the MT9D111 camera to transfer data between the device and memory of the CC3200 without CPU intervention. According to the documentation the micro-DMA controller provides the following features:

- 32-channel configurable DMA controller

- Support for memory-to-memory, memory-to-peripheral, and peripheral-to-memory in multiple transfer modes:

    - Basic for simple transfer scenarios

- Ping-pong for continuous data flow

- Scatter-gather for a programmable list of up to 256 arbitrary transfers initiated from a single request

- Highly flexible and configurable channel operation

  - Independently configured and operated channels

  - Dedicated channels for supported on-chip modules

  - One channel each for receive and transmit path for bidirectional modules

  - Dedicated channel for software-initiated transfers

  - Optional software-initiated requests for any channel

- Two levels of priority

- Design optimizations for improved bus access performance between DMA controller and the processor core:

  - DMA controller access is subordinate to core access

- Data sizes of 8, 16, and 32 bits

- Transfer size is programmable in binary steps from 1 to 1024

- Source and destination address increment size of byte, half-word, word, or no increment

- Interrupt on transfer completion, with a separate interrupt per channel

DMA Channels

The CC3200 has 32 DMA channels assigned to various peripherals. The table in Figure 7-4 highlights the DMA channel which is 22 that is used for the camera. The table was taken from the official documentation Figure 4-1 in the "Hardware Technical Reference Manual" for the CC3200. See Chapter 1 to find the download link for this PDF document.

DMACHMAPi Encoding	0
CH #	
0	GPTimer A0-A
1	GPTimer A0-B
2	GPTImer A1-A
3	GPTimer A1-B
4	GPTimer A2-A
5	GPTimer A2-B
6	GPTimer A3-A
7	GPTimer A3-B
8	UART A0 (RX)
9	UART A0 (TX)
10	UART A1 (RX)
11	UART A1 (TX)
12	LSPI(RX) (link)
13	LSPI(TX) (link)
14	ADC 0
15	ADC 2
16	ADC 4
17	ADC 6
18	GPIO A0
19	GPIO A1
20	GPIO A2
21	GPIO A3
22	Camera

Figure 7-4. The DMA channel for the camera

Each DMA channel has one or two control structures in a control table which is located in contiguous memory. The primary control structures for DMA channels 0 through 31 are listed first followed by the alternate control structures for the DMA channels 0 through 31. See Figure 7-5. Depending on the type of DMA transfer you may only need to use the primary control structures or both the primary control structures and the alternate control structures. For our camera project we will need to use both the primary and alternate control structures.

Offset	Channel
0x0	Channel 0 – primary
0x10	Channel 1 – primary
....	
0x1F0	Channel 31 – primary
0x200	Channel 0 – alternate
0x210	Channel 1 – alternate
....	
0x3F0	Channel 31 – alternate

Figure 7-5. The memory layout of the channel control table for DMA

The DMA control structure consists of a:

- Source End Pointer
- Destination End Pointer
- Control Word

- Reserved Area that is unused

See Figure 7-6.

Offset	Description
0x000	Source end pointer
0x004	Destination end pointer
0x008	Control word
0x00C	Reserved

Figure 7-6. The DMA control structure entry

The tDMAControlTable structure is the structure that defines an entry in the dma channel control table. These fields are used by the micro-DMA controller and normally it is not necessary for the user's software to directly read or write fields in the table. The structure is located in the udma.h source code file.

See Listing 7-8.

Listing 7-8. The tDMAControlTable structure that represents the micro-DMA control table

```
typedef struct

{

        //

        // The ending source address of the data transfer.

        //

        volatile void *pvSrcEndAddr;


        //

        // The ending destination address of the data transfer.

        //

        volatile void *pvDstEndAddr;


        //

        // The channel control mode.

        //

        volatile unsigned long ulControl;
```

```
    //

    // An unused location.

    //

    volatile unsigned long ulSpare;

}

tDMAControlTable;
```

DMA Ping Pong Mode

The type of DMA transfer mode we will use in this book for data transfer between the MT9D111 camera and the CC3200 device's memory will be the ping pong mode. The ping pong mode performs a continuous flow of data from the camera to the CC3200 device's memory. In order to use the ping pong mode both the primary and alternate control structures must be implemented.

The DMA ping pong mode transfer method does the following:

1. The DMA transfer is started by using the primary control structure to transfer data to buffer A.

2. After the data transfer is completed an interrupt is generated. The DMA controller modifies the control structure during the transfer of data and the data size at the end of the transfer will be set to 0. Thus, the control structure must be reloaded before the next data transfer.

3. The processor reloads in the data for the just completed control structure.

4. Next, the alternate control structure is read in and another transfer is started and data is transferred to buffer B.

5. When this transfer is finished another interrupt is generated which reloads the alternate control structure.

6. The data transfer using the primary control structure is then started and data is transferred to buffer A.

7. This data transfer cycle can repeat indefinitely.

See Figure 7-7.

228

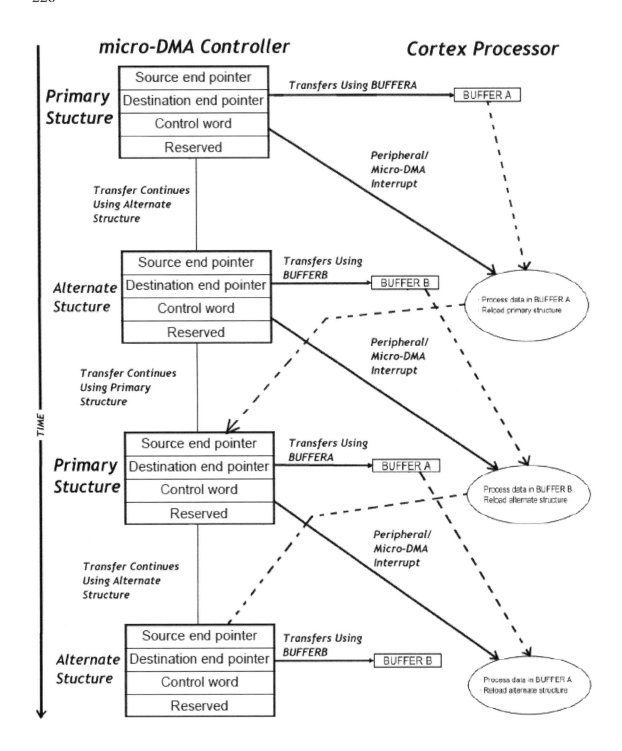

Figure 7-7. The ping pong DMA transfer mode

Note: The CC3200 SimpleLink Wi-Fi and Internet-of-Things Solution, a Single Chip Wireless MCU Technical Reference Manual contains key information regarding the CC3200's micro-DMA feature. This is a downloadable PDF file readable with Adobe Acrobat Reader which is a free program you can download for your computer.

Camera Interface Overview

The camera interface on the CC3200 has FIFO memory that is 32-bit wide and 64-locations deep. Data from the camera is put into this FIFO memory and then DMA interrupts are used to move this data from the FIFO to the CC3200 main memory. For more information on the camera's interface refer to the Hardware Technical Reference Manual. See Figure 7-8.

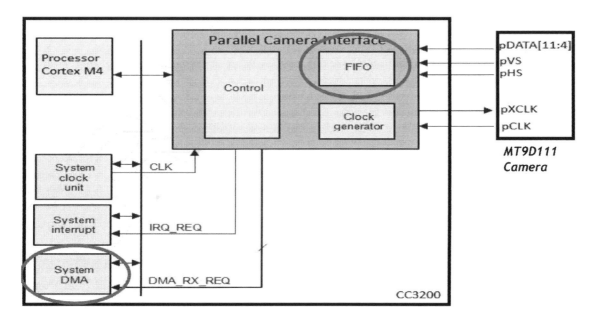

Figure 7-8. Parallel camera interface

The Camera Code

The camera related source code for the security system presented in this book is a modified version of the code for the websocket camera SDK example. The websocket camera SDK example provides a good starting point for developing camera projects for a CC3200 Simplelink device using a MT9D111 digital camera. Code to handle the operation of the MT9D111 can be found in the mt9d111.c file. The project for the websocket camera example is "websock_camera" in the official CC3200 SDK.

The InitCameraComponents() Function

The InitCameraComponents() function initializes the MT9D111 digital camera that is connected to the CC3200 through the parallel camera interface by doing the following:

1. Configures the parallel camera interface device pins by calling the PinMuxConfig() function.

2. Initialize I2C Interface by calling the I2CInit() function.

3. Initialize the camera micro-DMA interrupt controller by calling the CamControllerInit() function.

4. Initialize the camera sensor by calling the CameraSensorInit() function.

5. Start the camera in jpeg mode by calling the StartSensorInJpegMode(width, height) function with the width and height of the image to capture.

See Listing 7-9.

Listing 7-9. The InitCameraComponents() function

```
void InitCameraComponents(int width, int height)

{

        // Configure device pins

        PinMuxConfig();


        // Initialize I2C Interface

        I2CInit();


        // Initialize camera controller

        CamControllerInit();


        // Initialize camera sensor

        CameraSensorInit();


        #ifdef ENABLE_JPEG

                // Configure Sensor in Capture Mode

                PIXELS_IN_X_AXIS = width;

                PIXELS_IN_Y_AXIS = height;

                FRAME_SIZE_IN_BYTES = PIXELS_IN_X_AXIS * PIXELS_IN_Y_AXIS *
BYTES_PER_PIXEL;

                StartSensorInJpegMode(width, height);

        #endif

}
```

The PinMuxConfig() Function

The PinMuxConfig() function configures the pin connections on the CC3200 processor by doing the following:

1. Enables the UART by enabling the clock to the UART by calling the MAP_PRCMPeripheralClkEnable(PRCM_UARTA0, PRCM_RUN_MODE_CLK) function.

2. Configure the pins on the UART by calling the MAP_PinTypeUART(PIN_XX, PIN_MODE_X) function. The general format is that the first parameter is the pin number on the CC3200 chip and the second parameter is the mode to put that pin into.

3. Enables the camera for operation by calling the MAP_PRCMPeripheralClkEnable(PRCM_CAMERA, PRCM_RUN_MODE_CLK) function.

4. Enable the I2C interface on the CC3200 by calling the MAP_PRCMPeripheralClkEnable(PRCM_I2CA0, PRCM_RUN_MODE_CLK) function.

5. Configures the pins on the camera interface by calling the MAP_PinTypeCamera(PIN_XX, PIN_MODE_X) function. The first parameter is the pin number on the CC3200 chip to set. The second parameter is the mode to set the pin into.

6. Configures the pins for the I2C bus by calling the MAP_PinTypeI2C(PIN_XX, PIN_MODE_X) function. The first parameter is the pin number on the CC3200 chip to set. The second parameter is the mode to set the pin into.

> Important Note: The PinMuxConfig() function is generated by the TI PinMux program. The TI PinMux program is an interactive program where the user can add in components to a CC3200 based system and have the PinMuxConfig() function generated based on these components.

See Listing 7-10.

Listing 7-10. The PinMuxConfig() function

```
void PinMuxConfig(void)
{
    //
    // Enable Peripheral Clocks
    //
    MAP_PRCMPeripheralClkEnable(PRCM_UARTA0, PRCM_RUN_MODE_CLK);


    // PinMux 3.0 Uart, camera, and i2c
```

```
//

// Configure PIN_53 for UART0 UART0_TX

//

MAP_PinTypeUART(PIN_53, PIN_MODE_9);


//

// Configure PIN_57 for UART0 UART0_RX

//

MAP_PinTypeUART(PIN_57, PIN_MODE_3);


//////////////////////////////////////////////////////////////////

// From Websock Camera Example

//

// Enable Peripheral Clocks

//

MAP_PRCMPeripheralClkEnable(PRCM_CAMERA, PRCM_RUN_MODE_CLK);

MAP_PRCMPeripheralClkEnable(PRCM_I2CA0, PRCM_RUN_MODE_CLK);


//

// Configure PIN_55 for CAMERA0 CAM_pCLK

//

MAP_PinTypeCamera(PIN_55, PIN_MODE_4);


//

// Configure PIN_58 for CAMERA0 CAM_pDATA7

//

MAP_PinTypeCamera(PIN_58, PIN_MODE_4);


//
```

```
// Configure PIN_59 for CAMERA0 CAM_pDATA6

//

MAP_PinTypeCamera(PIN_59, PIN_MODE_4);


//

// Configure PIN_60 for CAMERA0 CAM_pDATA5

//

MAP_PinTypeCamera(PIN_60, PIN_MODE_4);


//

// Configure PIN_61 for CAMERA0 CAM_pDATA4

//

MAP_PinTypeCamera(PIN_61, PIN_MODE_4);


//

// Configure PIN_02 for CAMERA0 CAM_pXCLK

//

MAP_PinTypeCamera(PIN_02, PIN_MODE_4);


//

// Configure PIN_03 for CAMERA0 CAM_vS

//

MAP_PinTypeCamera(PIN_03, PIN_MODE_4);


//

// Configure PIN_04 for CAMERA0 CAM_hS

//

MAP_PinTypeCamera(PIN_04, PIN_MODE_4);
```

234

```
//
// Configure PIN_05 for CAMERA0 CAM_pDATA8
//
MAP_PinTypeCamera(PIN_05, PIN_MODE_4);


//
// Configure PIN_06 for CAMERA0 CAM_pDATA9
//
MAP_PinTypeCamera(PIN_06, PIN_MODE_4);


//
// Configure PIN_07 for CAMERA0 CAM_pDATA10
//
MAP_PinTypeCamera(PIN_07, PIN_MODE_4);


//
// Configure PIN_08 for CAMERA0 CAM_pDATA11
//
MAP_PinTypeCamera(PIN_08, PIN_MODE_4);


//
// Configure PIN_16 for I2C0 I2C_SCL
//
MAP_PinTypeI2C(PIN_16, PIN_MODE_9);


//
// Configure PIN_17 for I2C0 I2C_SDA
//
MAP_PinTypeI2C(PIN_17, PIN_MODE_9);
```

```
        //

        // Configure PIN_01 for MODE0

        //

        MAP_PinTypeI2C(PIN_01, PIN_MODE_0);

}
```

The I2Cinit() Function

The I2Cinit() initializes the I2C interface that is used with the camera by doing the following:

1. Enables the I2C interface by enabling the clock to the I2C interface.

2. Performs a software reset of the I2C interface.

3. Enables the I2C master block and sets the bus speed for the I2C.

See Listing 7-11.

Listing 7-11. The I2Cinit() function

```
unsigned long I2CInit()

{

        // Enable I2C Peripheral

        MAP_PRCMPeripheralClkEnable(PRCM_I2CA0, PRCM_RUN_MODE_CLK);

        MAP_PRCMPeripheralReset(PRCM_I2CA0);


        // Configure I2C module, 400 Kbps fast mode

        MAP_I2CMasterInitExpClk(I2CA0_BASE,80000000,false);


        return 0;

}
```

The CamControllerInit() Function

The CamControllerInit() function initializes the DMA control for the camera by doing the following:

1. Enables the clock for the camera.

2. Resets the camera.

3. Sets the input frequency for the camera module.

4. Resets the camera core.

5. Configure the camera parameters by calling the MAP_CameraParamsConfig(CAMERA_BASE, CAM_HS_POL_HI,CAM_VS_POL_HI, CAM_NOBT_SYNCHRO|CAM_IF_SYNCHRO|CAM_BT_CORRECT_EN) function. The first parameter is the base address of the camera module. The second parameter sets the HSync polarity.   The third parameter sets the VSync polarity. The last parameter holds the configuration flags.

6. Register a camera interrupt by calling the MAP_CameraIntRegister(CAMERA_BASE, CameraIntHandler) function. The first parameter is the camera's base address. The Second parameter is the name of the function that handles a DMA interrupt when data is being transferred from the camera to the CC3200 using micro-DMA.

7. The camera's internal clock divider is set by calling the MAP_CameraXClkConfig(CAMERA_BASE, 120000000,24000000) function. The first parameter is the base address of the camera module. The second parameter is the input to camera module. The final parameter defines the output required.

8. The camera's FIFO threshold for a DMA request is set by calling the MAP_CameraThresholdSet(CAMERA_BASE, 8) function. The first parameter is the base address of the camera module. The second parameter specifies the FIFO threshold. This function sets the FIFO threshold for DMA transfer request. The second parameter that specifies the threshold can range from 1 through 64.

9. Camera interrupts are enabled by calling the MAP_CameraIntEnable(CAMERA_BASE, CAM_INT_FE) function. The first parameter is the base address of the camera module. The second parameter indicates that the interrupt will occur at the end of the image frame after it is captured.

10. DMA transfers between the camera and the CC3200 are enabled by calling the MAP_CameraDMAEnable(CAMERA_BASE) function with the base address of the camera.

See Listing 7-12.

Listing 7-12. The CamControllerInit() function

```
static void CamControllerInit()

{

        MAP_PRCMPeripheralClkEnable(PRCM_CAMERA, PRCM_RUN_MODE_CLK);

        MAP_PRCMPeripheralReset(PRCM_CAMERA);


        #ifndef ENABLE_JPEG
```

```
                // Configure Camera clock

                // CamClkIn = ((240)/((1+1)+(1+1))) = 60 MHz

                PRCMCameraFreqSet(4, 2);
#else
                PRCMCameraFreqSet(2,1);
#endif


        MAP_CameraReset(CAMERA_BASE);


#ifndef ENABLE_JPEG
                MAP_CameraParamsConfig(CAMERA_BASE, CAM_HS_POL_HI, CAM_VS_POL_HI,
                                CAM_ORDERCAM_SWAP|CAM_NOBT_SYNCHRO);
#else
        MAP_CameraParamsConfig(CAMERA_BASE, CAM_HS_POL_HI,CAM_VS_POL_HI,
                                CAM_NOBT_SYNCHRO|CAM_IF_SYNCHRO|CAM_BT_CORRECT_EN);
#endif


        MAP_CameraIntRegister(CAMERA_BASE, CameraIntHandler);


#ifndef ENABLE_JPEG
                MAP_CameraXClkConfig(CAMERA_BASE, 60000000,3750000);
#else
                MAP_CameraXClkConfig(CAMERA_BASE, 120000000,24000000);
#endif


        MAP_CameraThresholdSet(CAMERA_BASE, 8);

        MAP_CameraIntEnable(CAMERA_BASE, CAM_INT_FE);

        MAP_CameraDMAEnable(CAMERA_BASE);

}
```

The CameraSensorInit() Function

The CameraSensorInit() function initializes the MT9D111 camera by writing to the required registers. See Listing 7-13.

Listing 7-13. The CameraSensorInit() function

```
long CameraSensorInit()

{

        long lRetVal = -1;


        lRetVal = RegLstWrite((s_RegList *)init_cmds_list, sizeof(init_cmds_list)/sizeof(s_RegList));

        ASSERT_ON_ERROR(lRetVal);



        #ifndef ENABLE_JPEG

                lRetVal = RegLstWrite((s_RegList *)preview_cmds_list,
sizeof(preview_cmds_list)/sizeof(s_RegList));

                ASSERT_ON_ERROR(lRetVal);

                lRetVal = RegLstWrite((s_RegList *)image_size_240_320_preview_cmds_list,
sizeof(image_size_240_320_preview_cmds_list)/ sizeof(s_RegList));

                ASSERT_ON_ERROR(lRetVal);

                lRetVal = RegLstWrite((s_RegList *)freq_setup_cmd_List,
sizeof(freq_setup_cmd_List)/sizeof(s_RegList));

                ASSERT_ON_ERROR(lRetVal);

                lRetVal = RegLstWrite((s_RegList *)preview_on_cmd_list,
sizeof(preview_on_cmd_list)/sizeof(s_RegList));

                ASSERT_ON_ERROR(lRetVal);

        #endif

        return 0;

}
```

The StartSensorInJpegMode() Function

The StartSensorInJpegMode() function initializes the MT9D111 camera in jpeg mode with the width and height specified in the input parameters by setting the required registers in the camera. See Listing 7-14.

Listing 7-14. The StartSensorInJpegMode() function

```c
long StartSensorInJpegMode(int width, int height)

{

        #ifdef ENABLE_JPEG

                long lRetVal = -1;


                lRetVal = RegLstWrite((s_RegList *)capture_cmds_list,
sizeof(capture_cmds_list)/sizeof(s_RegList));

                ASSERT_ON_ERROR(lRetVal);


                resolution_cmds_list[INDEX_SIZE_WIDTH].usValue = width;

                resolution_cmds_list[INDEX_SIZE_HEIGHT].usValue = height;

                lRetVal = RegLstWrite((s_RegList *)resolution_cmds_list,
sizeof(resolution_cmds_list)/sizeof(s_RegList));

                ASSERT_ON_ERROR(lRetVal);


                lRetVal = RegLstWrite((s_RegList *)start_jpeg_capture_cmd_list,
sizeof(start_jpeg_capture_cmd_list)/sizeof(s_RegList));

                ASSERT_ON_ERROR(lRetVal);

        #endif

        return 0;

}
```

Important Note: Since this is a quick start guide to using the MT9D111 camera I won't go into detail of the inner workings of the camera. The source code for the camera which is in the "mt9d111.c" file which contains the key functions that you will need to use the camera. This source code file is part of the standard CC3200 SDK and is used in the websocket camera example. Also, a key piece of documentation is the CC3200 Peripheral Driver Library User's Guide which is an executable help file that is located in the docs directory of the SDK distribution. This guide defines all the MAP functions that are actually implemented in the CC3200's device's ROM (read only memory).

The StartCamera() Function

The StartCamera() function captures an image from the MT9D111 camera. A pointer to a pointer to the image data is returned through the WriteBuffer input parameter and the length of the image is returned.

See Listing 7-15.

Listing 7-15. The StartCamera() function

```
unsigned short StartCamera(char **WriteBuffer)

{

        unsigned short Writelength;

        //

        // Waits in the below loop till Capture button is pressed

        //

        Writelength = CaptureImage(WriteBuffer);


        return(Writelength);

}
```

The CaptureImage() Function

The CaptureImage() function captures an image with the MT9D111 camera.

The image is stored in the g_image variable which is a structure that contains a jpeg header followed by the jpeg data. The maximum size allocated for the jpeg image is 70k.

The SMTP_BUF_LEN is the length of the buffer that holds that jpeg header.

```
#define SMTP_BUF_LEN            1024
```

The define ONE_KB represents 1 kilo byte.

```
#define ONE_KB             (1024)
```

The IMAGE_BUF_SIZE is the size of the image buffer that holds the image data for the captured jpeg image.

```
#define IMAGE_BUF_SIZE          ROBS_IMAGE_BUF_SIZE
```

The NUM_OF_4B_CHUNKS is the number of unsigned long integers that are in the image data buffer.

#define NUM_OF_4B_CHUNKS   ROBS_NUM_OF_4B_CHUNKS

The ROBS_NUM_OF_1KB_BUFFERS is the number of 1k blocks that are in the image data buffer.

#define ROBS_NUM_OF_1KB_BUFFERS   70

The ROBS_IMAGE_BUF_SIZE is the size of the image data buffer

#define ROBS_IMAGE_BUF_SIZE   (ONE_KB * ROBS_NUM_OF_1KB_BUFFERS)

The ROBS_NUM_OF_4B_CHUNKS is the number of unsigned long integers that can be contained within the image buffer.

#define ROBS_NUM_OF_4B_CHUNKS   ((ROBS_IMAGE_BUF_SIZE)/(sizeof(unsigned long)))

The ImageBuffer structure holds the jpeg header and the jpeg image data for the picture that is taken by the MT9D111 camera.

```
struct ImageBuffer

{

        #ifdef ENABLE_JPEG

                char g_header[SMTP_BUF_LEN] /*= {'\0'}*/;

        #endif

        unsigned long g_image_buffer[NUM_OF_4B_CHUNKS];

};
```

The g_image variable is an ImageBuffer structure that is the buffer that holds the jpeg header and the jpeg image data.

```
struct ImageBuffer g_image;
```

The CaptureImage() function does the following:

1. The DMA is configured for transferring images between the MT9D111 camera and the CC3200 device by calling the DMAConfig() function.

2. The image capture is started by calling the MAP_CameraCaptureStart(CAMERA_BASE) function with the camera's base address as the parameter.

3. Wait while the frame is being captured. During this period g_frame_end will be 0.

4. The image capture is stopped immediately by calling the MAP_CameraCaptureStop(CAMERA_BASE, true) function. The base address of the camera is the first parameter. The second parameter which is true indicates that the capture will be stopped immediately instead of waiting till the end of the frame.

5. Create the jpeg header for the captured image by calling the CreateJpegHeader() function.

242

6. Modify the jpeg header so that the jpeg header and the image data are continuous in the array.

7. Set the WriteBuffer variable to the jpeg header which is the start of the jpeg image.

8. Return the total size of the jpeg image which is the size of the jpeg header and the jpeg image data.

See Listing 7-16.

Listing 7-16. The CaptureImage() function

```
static unsigned short CaptureImage(char** WriteBuffer)

{

        //

        // Configure DMA in ping-pong mode

        //

        DMAConfig();


        //

        // Perform Image Capture

        //

        MAP_CameraCaptureStart(CAMERA_BASE);

        while(g_frame_end == 0);

        MAP_CameraCaptureStop(CAMERA_BASE, true);


        //

        // Create JPEG Header

        //

        #ifdef ENABLE_JPEG

                memset(g_image.g_header, '\0', sizeof(g_image.g_header));

                g_header_length = CreateJpegHeader((char *)&(g_image.g_header[0]), PIXELS_IN_X_AXIS,
PIXELS_IN_Y_AXIS, 0, 0x0020, 9);
```

```
        // This loop pushes the header to the end of the array so that the entire picture can be contiguous in
memory

        unsigned short shift;

        for(shift=1, shift <= g_header_length; shift++)

        {

                g_image.g_header[SMTP_BUF_LEN - shift] = g_image.g_header[g_header_length -
shift];

        }

    #endif

    *WriteBuffer = &(g_image.g_header[SMTP_BUF_LEN - g_header_length]);


    return(g_header_length + g_frame_size_in_bytes);

}
```

The DMAConfig() Function

The DMAConfig() function configures the DMA for transferring data from the MT9D111 camera to the CC3200 device.

The p_buffer variable is a pointer to an unsigned long integer that represents the buffer for the jpeg's image data. This is used to set the new destination address for the image data as it is read in using DMA.

```
static unsigned long *p_buffer = NULL;
```

The DMAConfig() function does the following:

1. Clears the image buffer data array.

2. Points the p_buffer variable to the start of the jpeg image data buffer array.

3. Initialize the micro-DMA for ping pong DMA transfer by calling the UDMAInit() function.

4. Set up the DMA transfer in ping pong mode for the primary control structure by calling the UDMASetupTransfer() function with the UDMA_CH22_CAMERA as the first parameter to set the primary channel for the camera and UDMA_MODE_PINGPONG as the second parameter to set the DMA transfer type.

5. Increase the p_buffer pointer which points to the destination of the next group of bytes from the DMA transfer. This buffer is the alternate buffer.

6. Set up the DMA transfer in ping pong mode for the alternate control structure by calling the UDMASetupTransfer() function with the UDMA_CH22_CAMERA|UDMA_ALT_SELECT as the first parameter to set the alternate channel for the camera and UDMA_MODE_PINGPONG as the second parameter to set the DMA transfer type.

7. Increase the p_buffer pointer which points to the destination of the next group of bytes from the DMA transfer. This buffer is the primary buffer.

8. Initialize variables relating to the DMA transfer of data.

9. Clear any pending interrupt from a DMA transfer being completed by calling the CameraIntClear(CAMERA_BASE,CAM_INT_DMA) function.

10. Enables the DMA done interrupt source by calling the CameraIntEnable(CAMERA_BASE,CAM_INT_DMA) function. The interrupt handler will be called when a DMA transfer is completed.

See Listing 7-17

Listing 7-17. The DMAConfig() function

```
static void DMAConfig()

{

        memset(g_image.g_image_buffer,0xF80F,sizeof(g_image.g_image_buffer));

        p_buffer = &(g_image.g_image_buffer[0]);

        //

        // Initilalize DMA

        //

        UDMAInit();

        //

        // Setup ping-pong transfer

        //

        UDMASetupTransfer(UDMA_CH22_CAMERA,UDMA_MODE_PINGPONG,TOTAL_DMA_ELEMENT
        S,UDMA_SIZE_32, UDMA_ARB_8,(void *)CAM_BUFFER_ADDR, UDMA_SRC_INC_32, (void
        *)p_buffer, UDMA_DST_INC_32);

        //

        // Pong Buffer

        //

        p_buffer += TOTAL_DMA_ELEMENTS;

        UDMASetupTransfer(UDMA_CH22_CAMERA|UDMA_ALT_SELECT,UDMA_MODE_PINGPONG,TO
        TAL_DMA_ELEMENTS, UDMA_SIZE_32, UDMA_ARB_8,(void *)CAM_BUFFER_ADDR,
        UDMA_SRC_INC_32, (void *)p_buffer, UDMA_DST_INC_32);
```

```
    //

    //  Ping Buffer

    //

    p_buffer += TOTAL_DMA_ELEMENTS;


    g_dma_txn_done = 0;

    g_frame_size_in_bytes = 0;

    g_frame_end = 0;

    g_total_dma_intrpts = 0;


    //

    // Clear any pending interrupt

    //

    CameraIntClear(CAMERA_BASE,CAM_INT_DMA);


    //

    // DMA Interrupt unmask from apps config

    //

    CameraIntEnable(CAMERA_BASE,CAM_INT_DMA);

}
```

The UDMAInit() Function

The UDMAInit() function initializes the micro-DMA on the CC3200 device by doing the following:

1. Enable the clock for the micro-DMA on the CC3200 device.

2. Reset the micro-DMA.

3. Register the interrupt handlers.

4. Enables the micro-DMA controller by calling the MAP_uDMAEnable() function. The DMA controller must be enabled before it can be configured or used.

5. The DMA channel control table is initialized to 0.

6. The base address of the DMA channel control table is set by calling the MAP_uDMAControlBaseSet(gpCtlTbl) function. The control table is gpCtlTbl and is an array of 64 elements of tDMAControlTable. The tDMAControlTable structure is defined in Listing 7-8.

7. Reset application callbacks.

See Listing 7-18.

Listing 7-18. The UDMAInit() function

```
void UDMAInit()

{

        unsigned int uiLoopCnt;


        //

        // Enable McASP at the PRCM module

        //

        MAP_PRCMPeripheralClkEnable(PRCM_UDMA,PRCM_RUN_MODE_CLK);

        MAP_PRCMPeripheralReset(PRCM_UDMA);


        //

        // Register interrupt handlers

        //

#if defined(USE_TIRTOS) || defined(USE_FREERTOS) || defined(SL_PLATFORM_MULTI_THREADED)

                // USE_TIRTOS: if app uses TI-RTOS (either networking/non-networking)

                // USE_FREERTOS: if app uses Free-RTOS (either networking/non-networking)

                // SL_PLATFORM_MULTI_THREADED: if app uses any OS + networking(simplelink)

                osi_InterruptRegister(INT_UDMA, DmaSwIntHandler, INT_PRIORITY_LVL_1);

                osi_InterruptRegister(INT_UDMAERR, DmaErrorIntHandler, INT_PRIORITY_LVL_1);

#else

                MAP_IntPrioritySet(INT_UDMA, INT_PRIORITY_LVL_1);

                MAP_uDMAIntRegister(UDMA_INT_SW, DmaSwIntHandler);
```

```
                MAP_IntPrioritySet(INT_UDMAERR, INT_PRIORITY_LVL_1);

                MAP_uDMAIntRegister(UDMA_INT_ERR, DmaErrorIntHandler);

    #endif


        //

        // Enable uDMA using master enable

        //

        MAP_uDMAEnable();


        //

        // Set Control Table

        //

        memset(gpCtlTbl,0,sizeof(tDMAControlTable)*CTL_TBL_SIZE);

        MAP_uDMAControlBaseSet(gpCtlTbl);


        //

        // Reset App Callbacks

        //

        for(uiLoopCnt = 0; uiLoopCnt < MAX_NUM_CH; uiLoopCnt++)

        {

                gfpAppCallbackHndl[uiLoopCnt] = NULL;

        }

    }
```

The UDMASetupTransfer() Function

The UDMASetupTransfer() function sets up the actual DMA transfer from the source buffer to the destination buffer using the specified DMA transfer mode in this case the ping pong mode designed for continuous data transfer.

The function does the following:

1. Sets the DMA control parameters.

2. Enable attributes of the DMA channel.

3. Sets the transfer parameters for the DMA channel.

4. Enables the DMA channel for operation.

See Listing 7-19.

Listing 7-19. The UDMASetupTransfer() function

```
void UDMASetupTransfer(unsigned long ulChannel, unsigned long ulMode,

                unsigned long ulItemCount, unsigned long ulItemSize,

                unsigned long ulArbSize, void *pvSrcBuf,

                unsigned long ulSrcInc, void *pvDstBuf,

                unsigned long ulDstInc)

{

        MAP_uDMAChannelControlSet(ulChannel, ulItemSize | ulSrcInc | ulDstInc | ulArbSize);

        MAP_uDMAChannelAttributeEnable(ulChannel,UDMA_ATTR_USEBURST);

        MAP_uDMAChannelTransferSet(ulChannel, ulMode, pvSrcBuf, pvDstBuf, ulItemCount);

        MAP_uDMAChannelEnable(ulChannel);

}
```

The Camera DMA Interrupt Handler Code

The CameraIntHandler() function handles interrupts generated from the camera and is called when each DMA transfer from the camera has completed and is used to set up the next DMA transfer in ping pong mode with either the primary control structure or the alternative control structure used to control the transfer and using either the primary buffer or alternate buffer to store the incoming data from the camera. This interrupt is also called if the camera has finished capturing the entire image.

The function does the following:

1. If there has been more than one DMA interrupt and the image frame has finished being captured then

    1. Clear the end frame interrupt source which resets it and allows it to be triggered again.

    2. Set the g_frame_end to 1 which indicates that a complete image frame has been captured.

3. Stop the camera from capturing another frame immediately.

2. If a DMA transfer has finished then do the following:

   1. Clears the DMA transfer finished interrupt source which resets the interrupt to be triggered again.

   2. Increase the number of DMA interrupts completed by incrementing by 1 the g_total_dma_intrpts variable.

   3. Update the current frame size that has been processed based on the completed DMA transfer and storing this value in the g_frame_size_in_bytes variable.

   4. If the current size of the processed frame is less than the maximum frame size and also less than the size of the image data buffer then do the following:

      1. If the g_dma_txn_done variable is 0 then set up a new DMA transfer using the primary buffer. Increase the p_buffer pointer to point to the alternate buffer in preparation for the next DMA ping pong transfer. Set the g_dma_txn_done variable to 1.

      2. If the g_dma_txn_done variable is not equal to 0 then set up a new DMA transfer using the alternate buffer. Increase the p_buffer pointer to point to the primary buffer in preparation for the next DMA ping pong transfer. Set the g_dma_txn_done variable to 0.

   5. Otherwise if the conditions in Step 4 are not met then do the following instead:

      1. Halt execution of the program for a small amount of time.

      2. Disable the DMA channel to the camera.

      3. Disable the camera interrupt source that triggers an interrupt on the completion of a DMA transfer.

      4. Set the g_frame_end variable to 1 to indicate that an entire frame has been captured and is ready for transmission

See Listing 7-20.

Listing 7-20. The CameraIntHandler() function

```
static void CameraIntHandler()

{

        if(g_total_dma_intrpts > 1 && MAP_CameraIntStatus(CAMERA_BASE) & CAM_INT_FE)

        {

                MAP_CameraIntClear(CAMERA_BASE, CAM_INT_FE);

                g_frame_end = 1;
```

250

```c
            MAP_CameraCaptureStop(CAMERA_BASE, true);

    }


    if(CameraIntStatus(CAMERA_BASE)& CAM_INT_DMA)

    {
            // Camera DMA Done clear

            CameraIntClear(CAMERA_BASE,CAM_INT_DMA);


            g_total_dma_intrpts++;

            g_frame_size_in_bytes += (TOTAL_DMA_ELEMENTS*sizeof(unsigned long));

            if(g_frame_size_in_bytes < FRAME_SIZE_IN_BYTES && g_frame_size_in_bytes <
IMAGE_BUF_SIZE)

            {
                    if(g_dma_txn_done == 0)

                    {

                            UDMASetupTransfer(UDMA_CH22_CAMERA,UDMA_MODE_PINGPON
                            G,TOTAL_DMA_ELEMENTS,UDMA_SIZE_32, UDMA_ARB_8,(void
                            *)CAM_BUFFER_ADDR, UDMA_SRC_INC_32, (void *)p_buffer,
                            UDMA_DST_INC_32);

                            p_buffer += TOTAL_DMA_ELEMENTS;

                            g_dma_txn_done = 1;

                    }
                    else

                    {

                            UDMASetupTransfer(UDMA_CH22_CAMERA|UDMA_ALT_SELECT,UD
                            MA_MODE_PINGPONG,TOTAL_DMA_ELEMENTS, UDMA_SIZE_32,
                            UDMA_ARB_8,(void *)CAM_BUFFER_ADDR, UDMA_SRC_INC_32,
                            (void *)p_buffer, UDMA_DST_INC_32);

                            p_buffer += TOTAL_DMA_ELEMENTS;

                            g_dma_txn_done = 0;

                    }

            }
```

```
        else

        {

            // Disable DMA

            MAP_UtilsDelay(20000);

            MAP_uDMAChannelDisable(UDMA_CH22_CAMERA);

            CameraIntDisable(CAMERA_BASE,CAM_INT_DMA);

            g_frame_end = 1;

        }

    }

}
```

The MT9D111 I2C Address

For the MT9111 camera there are two possible addresses for the I2C. The I2C address can be either 0xBA or 0x90. The MT9D111 camera made by ArduCAM has the 0x90 address.

You would define the I2C address in the "mt9d111.c" source file such as:

#define CAM_I2C_SLAVE_ADDR   ((0xBA >> 1))

or

// ArduCAM's MT9D111

#define CAM_I2C_SLAVE_ADDR   ((0x90 >> 1))

The Memory Management File

The CC3200 device has a maximum of about 240K for application code and data.

The "cc3200v1p32.cmd" file contains the memory management file. The key change I made in the default file is to increase the amount of room for data that is allocated. This is due to the greater space needed in the CC3200 main memory to store the incoming jpeg image from the camera. Depending on the complexity of the image you want to capture you may need to increase the size of the allocation. See my changes in bold in Listing 7-21.

Listing 7-21. The memory management file for the CC3200

//***

// The starting address of the application. Normally the interrupt vectors

252

// must be located at the beginning of the application.

//**

#define RAM_BASE 0x20004000

/* System memory map */

MEMORY

{

  /* Application uses internal RAM for program and data */

  // 0x13000 = 77824 decimal

  SRAM_CODE (RWX) : origin = 0x20004000, length = 0x13000

  //SRAM_DATA (RWX) : origin = 0x20017000, length = 0x19000

  // 0x21B00 = 137984 decimal

  SRAM_DATA (RWX) : origin = 0x20017000, length = 0x21B00

}

/* Section allocation in memory */

SECTIONS

{

  .intvecs: > RAM_BASE

  .init_array : > SRAM_CODE

  .vtable : > SRAM_CODE

  .text : > SRAM_CODE

  .const : > SRAM_CODE

  .cinit : > SRAM_CODE

  .pinit : > SRAM_CODE

  .data : > SRAM_DATA

```
.bss   :  > SRAM_DATA

.sysmem :  > SRAM_DATA

.stack  :  > SRAM_DATA(HIGH)

}
```

Summary

In this chapter I discussed the CC3200 device portion of the home security system I cover in this book. I start with an overview of the key functional components of the CC3200 device. I then cover source code related to the TCP server which is used to process incoming Android commands and return the requested image data. Next, I discuss the CC3200's DMA or direct memory access system called micro-DMA. The camera interface that is used to connect the camera to the CC3200 device is then discussed. Finally, I cover the important camera related source code that is used to capture and transfer an image from the camera to the CC3200 device's main memory and then from the main memory to the Android device using wifi.

Chapter 8

Hands on Example: Building an Android and TI CC3200 Security System

In this chapter I present a quick start guide to setting up and operating the GotchaCAM home security system discussed in this book.

General Overview of the GotchaCAM Alarm System

The GotchaCAM alarm system consists of:

1. An ArduCAM CC3200 Uno or a TI CC3200 Launchpad.

2. A TI Camera Boosterpack (CC3200CAMBOOST) if you are using a TI CC3200 Launchpad. The ArduCAM CC3200 Uno has a built in camera interface.

3. A MT9D111 digital camera.

4. An Android phone with an operating system of 2.2 or higher.

An overview of the alarm system is shown in Figure 8-1. For a more detailed explanation of how the system works please see Chapter 6 and Chapter 7. The alarm system has code that needs to be installed on the CC3200 device and the Android device in order for the system to work correctly.

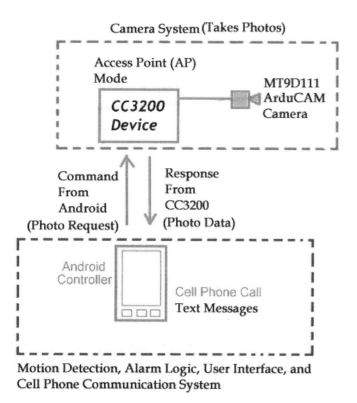

Figure 8-1. GotchaCAM system overview

Official Support Web Site

The official support web site for this book is located at:

http://www.psycho-sphere.com/cc3200diy.html

There you will find the binaries and project files for this book.

Important Note: The license for this source code is for non-commercial use only. Use of this code in a commercial alarm system that is being sold is prohibited.

PROGRAM FILES:

GotchaCAM Android APK file:

http://www.psycho-sphere.com/GotchaCAMV10.apk

GotchaCAM Android APK file (Zipped):

http://www.psycho-sphere.com/GotchaCAMAPKV10.zip

CC3200 Binary Program file:

http://www.psycho-sphere.com/CC3200GotchaCAMBinary.zip

SOURCE CODE FILES:

GotchaCAM Android Source Code:

http://www.psycho-sphere.com/AndroidGotchaCAMV10.zip

GotchaCAM CC3200 Source Code:

http://www.psycho-sphere.com/CC3200GotchaCAMV10.zip

Downloading and Installing the CC3200 SDK

The web page for the CC3200 SDK download and the CC3200 SDK Service Pack is located at:

http://www.ti.com/tool/cc3200sdk

The service pack should already be installed on your device however, if it is not you will need to install it using the Uniflash program by clicking on the "Service Pack Programming" button on the main menu. The SDK contains drivers for the CC3200 device that you will need to install on your development system so that the computer will recognize the CC3200 device when you connect it to the computer's USB port. See Chapter 1 for more detailed information.

Downloading and Installing TI Code Composer Studio

The TI Code Composer Studio also contains drivers for the CC3200. If the CC3200 device is not recognized by your computer after installing the SDK then try to install the TI Code Composer Studio on your development system to see if that solves the problem. See Chapter 1 for more detailed information.

Downloading and Installing Uniflash

The Uniflash download web site is at:

http://www.ti.com/tool/uniflash

The Uniflash tool is the one you will need to actually write the CC3200 binary file to the CC3200 device. See Chapter 1 for more detailed information.

Installing the CC3200 Binary File

The binary file that needs to be written to the CC3200 device is located at:

http://www.psycho-sphere.com/CC3200GotchaCAMBinary.zip

The CC3200 project source code is located at:

http://www.psycho-sphere.com/CC3200GotchaCAMV10.zip

You can unzip a .zip file using 7-zip which is a free public compression/uncompression program located at:

http://www.7-zip.org

The uncompressed binary image file should have a .bin extension and it is this file that needs to be written to the CC3200 device.

Assuming the CC3200 flash memory has been formatted and the service pack is installed you can proceed with installing the binary file to the CC3200 device using Uniflash. This binary file is the MCU image that needs to be written to the CC3200. Refer to the "Hands on Example" in Chapter 1 on how to install an MCU file on the CC3200.

You can also use the TI Code Composer Studio to generate the binary file from the source code and then have that binary file written to the CC3200 device using Uniflash. You will also need to import and build the "ti_rtos_config" project that is needed for the main project. Again, please refer to the "Hands on Example" in Chapter 1.

Important Note: Make sure the camera or booster pack is NOT attached to the CC3200 device and the jumpers are set correctly for your CC3200 device for writing the program image.

Installing the Android Application APK

The Android application APK can be downloaded in both APK format and zipped APK format.

The APK format is located at:

http://www.psycho-sphere.com/GotchaCAMV10.apk

The zipped APK format is located at:

http://www.psycho-sphere.com/GotchaCAMAPKV10.zip

Install this APK file just as you would any other APK file. However, you may need to go under Settings->Applications and check the option to allow the installation of applications from non-Google store sources.

You can also install the Android application by downloading the Eclipse ADT Bundle version of the project source code at:

http://www.psycho-sphere.com/AndroidGotchaCAMV10.zip

You will need to unzip the source code and compile and install it using the Android ADT Bundle or the newer Android Studio.

Putting the Camera on the ArduCAM CC3200 UNO

After writing the binary image file to the CC3200 device you will need to put the MT9D111 camera into the camera interface before you start using your new security system. The camera is aligned so that the leftmost pins on the left side of the camera fit into the leftmost holes on the camera interface. There should be two columns of pins on the rightmost side of the camera that are not used and are outside the camera interface. See Figure 8-2.

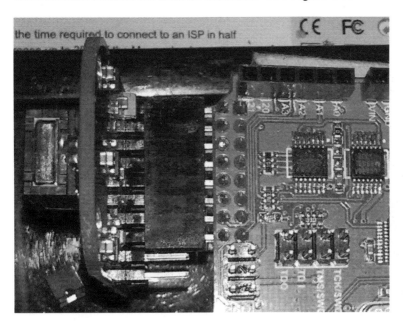

Figure 8-2. Camera placement on the ArduCAM CC3200 Uno

Quick Start Guide to Setting Up and Operating the GotchaCAM Alarm System

1. Download and install the CC3200 SDK which contains the drivers for the CC3200 device.

2. Connect your CC3200 device to your development system to complete the installation of the drivers and to verify that the drivers are working. For the ArduCAM CC3200 Uno you will need a mini usb to regular USB cable.

3. The TI Code Composer Studio also contains drivers for the CC3200 device. If you can't get your development system to recognize the CC3200 then try to install TI Code Composer Studio. You will also need the TI Code Composer Studio if you want to modify the source code for this project.

4. Download and install Uniflash on your development system.

5. Download and unzip the CC3200 binary file from the project web site.

6. Write the binary to the CC3200 using Uniflash. See Chapter 1 for more details on to how to do this.

7. Download and install the Android APK on your Android phone.

8. Make sure the MT9D111 camera is connected to the camera interface and plug in the CC3200 device into your computer's USB port.

9. Go to your Android device's Settings→Wifi section and turn on the wifi. You should see a new access point called "GotchaCAM" which is the CC3200 device that has been placed into access point mode. Connect the Android device to this access point. See Figure 8-3.

Figure 8-3. Starting up the Android app

10. Start up the GotchaCAM Android application you just installed. The following screen should appear. See Figure 8-4.

260

Figure 8-4. Start up screen

11. The first thing you need to do is specify a phone number that will receive emergency call outs and emergency text messages to indicate that an intruder has been detected. Click on the top edit text box and enter the phone number using the Android's keyboard that should pop up. See Figure 8-5.

Figure 8-5. The Android keyboard

12. Next, click on the "Done" key to enter the phone number as the emergency call out phone number. A toast pop up message should also be displayed confirming that the number has been changed. See Figure 8-6.

Figure 8-6. Changing the emergency phone number

13. Press the Android's menu key to bring up the menus. The menus for this application are shown in Figure 8-7 and Figure 8-8.

Figure 8-7. GotchaCAM app's menus

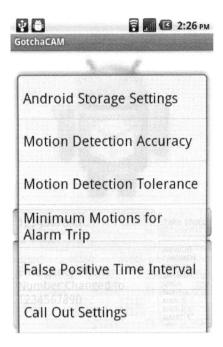

Figure 8-8. GotchaCAM app's menus

14. Select the "Surveillance" menu and then select the "Turn on Surveillance" option. See Figure 8-9. This continuously displays images from the camera.

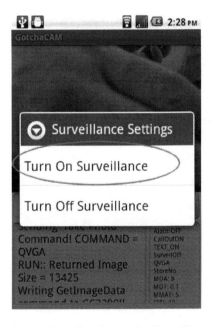

Figure 8-9. Turning on the Surveillance

15. When the surveillance is turned on you should see a continuous series of images from the camera as well as a frame number that continually increases. See Figure 8-10.

Figure 8-10. Real Time Surveillance

16. Under the "Alarm Settings" menu select the "Activate Alarm" setting. See Figure 8-11.

Figure 8-11. Activating the alarm

17. You should see a toast popup that indicates that the Alarm is now active and then the alarm calibration will start. Once the calibration has finished the alarm will be armed and the camera will detect motion. In the lower debug window you should see the current frame number since the beginning of surveillance. You should see the current SAD value which measures the differences between the current frame and the last frame. The next entry should be the SAD threshold. If the current SAD value is greater than the SAD threshold then a motion has been detected. The last entry is the number of motions that have been

detected in the false positive time interval. If the number of motions is equal to or greater than the minimum number of motions required to trip the alarm then the alarm is triggered. The minimum number of motions must occur within the false positive time interval which is also set by the user. See Figure 8-12.

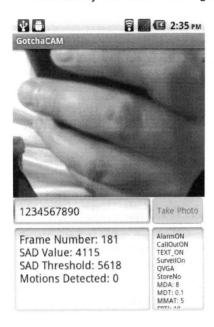

Figure 8-12. The alarm is now armed.

18. Trip the camera's motion detection logic by moving an object around in front of the camera until the alarm is tripped. You should see a "ALARM TRIPPED!!!" message in the debug window when this happens. See Figure 8-13.

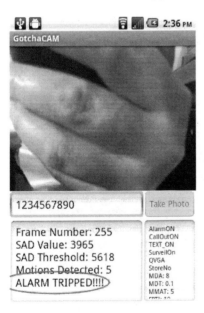

Figure 8-13. Alarm is tripped

19. By default the emergency call out and the emergency text message is sent out and you should see a screen similar to that shown in Figure 8-14 that notifies you that the phone is making a call to the designated emergency phone number and sending out an emergency text message.

Figure 8-14.

20. You can also save incoming images where motion is detected by selecting "Save Incoming Images" under the "Android Storage Settings" menu item. See Figure 8-15.

Figure 8-15. Saving incoming images to local Android storage

21. Turn off the alarm and the surveillance. You can take a single photos by pressing the "Take Photo" button. If you have "Save incoming images" turned on then these photos will be saved to the Android's file system. See Figure 8-16

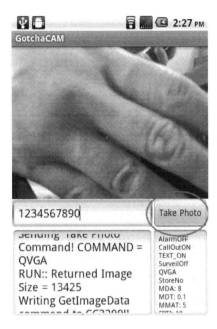

Figure 8-16. Taking single photos

22. You can load in saved images and display them inside the application by selecting the "Load Stored Image" menu item and then selecting the stored image to display. When using surveillance the only frames that are saved are those that occur when the alarm has been set and has been tripped and motion is detected. See Figure 8-17.

Figure 8-17. Loaded stored image

Application Settings

- Alarm Settings – Turns the alarm system on or off.

- Text Message Settings – Turns the emergency text message alert system on or off.

- Resolution Settings – Sets the resolution at which to capture images using the MT9D111 camera that is attached to the CC3200 device. The available resolutions are VGA, QVGA, and QQVGA. Note that if a scene is too complex then VGA resolution may not work correctly due to the limited memory of the CC3200 device in which to store that image.

- Surveillance Settings – Turns the surveillance feature on or off. The surveillance continuously captures images from the camera.

- Load Stored Image – Displays a list of saved jpeg picture files that are in the "CAMPics" directory under the Android's "Pictures" directory.

- Android Storage Settings – Turns the saving of incoming images from the camera on or off.

- Motion Detection Accuracy – Sets the accuracy of the motion detection method. For example, if this value is 8 then every eighth pixel in the image is tested for motion. The lower the number the higher the accuracy.

- Motion Detection Tolerance – Sets the tolerance of the motion detection method. This sets the percentage above the SAD threshold value where a SAD value reading would denote that a motion has been detected.

- Minimum Motion for Alarm Trip – Sets the minimum number of motions that need to be detected for the alarm to trip.

- False Positive Time Interval – Sets the time interval where the alarm can be tripped if the minimum number of motions has been detected.

- Call out Settings – Turns on or off the emergency call out when an intruder is detected and the alarm is tripped.

The Emergency Text Message

The emergency text message alert sent out by the GotchaCAM security system is shown in Figure 8-18. During testing I sent the emergency text alert messages to the same phone that I was running the application on. Under the "Messaging" application the text message that I sent is on the right hand side and the text message I received on the left hand side. In both cases the message was alerting me that the alarm has been tripped and the number of motions that were detected that caused it to trip.

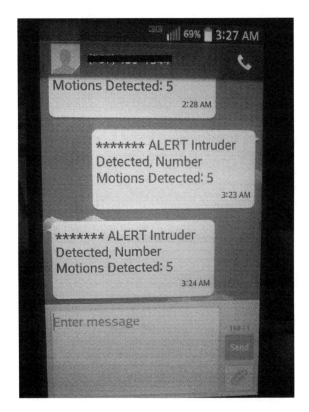

Figure 8-18. The emergency text message alert

Chapter 9

Deploying your GotchaCAM Wireless Intruder Alarm and Surveillance System

In this chapter I cover deployment related information regarding the GotchaCAM security and surveillance system. This system consists of an Android cell phone or tablet and a CC3200 device such as an ArduCAM CC3200 Uno (recommended) or a TI CC3200 Launchpad with a TI Camera Booster Pack and an MT9D111 digital camera.

The Android Controller

An Android cell phone with operating system version 2.2 (Froyo) or above should work with the GotchaCAM security and surveillance system presented in this book. There are many inexpensive no contract prepaid Android cell phones available. The latest Android operating system version available as this book is written is 6.0 (Marshmallow).

Many Android cell phones are prepaid cell phones where there is no long term contract and the cell phone can be used on a month to month basis with no credit check or other disclosure of private information. The cell phone can be activated using prepaid cards from the mobile phone service provider that can be bought from many retail stores or online from Amazon.com. The cost of the phone itself can be very inexpensive depending on the phone. The phone service itself is prepaid which means that you will need to pay the provider before you use the phone to make a call out or to send a text message out.

Once example of an inexpensive Android phone is the LG Tribute 2 prepaid phone from Virgin Mobile that sells on Amazon for approximately $40-$50 USD. This phone has version 5.1 (Lollipop) of the Android operating system installed on it.

The ArduCAM CC3200 Uno DIY Wifi Security Spy Ghost Hunter Camera Starter Kit

If you are just starting in CC3200 development or you are deploying your new GotchaCAM alarm system then I recommend you purchase the ArduCAM CC3200 Uno DIY Wifi Security Spy Ghost Hunter Camera Starter Kit that has everything that you need to start developing a wifi camera based security system project as well as everything you will need to deploy it in your home. This kit should be available soon on Amazon.com or on Ebay from ArduCAM.

This kit is to contain:

- 1 ArduCAM CC3200 Uno Board

- 1 ArduCAM MT9D111 Camera Module

- 1 Mini USB Cable

- 1 AC Power Adapter

- 1 ArduCAM CC3200 Uno Board Plastic Case

The ArduCAM CC3200 Uno Board Plastic Case

At the very minimum I recommend purchasing a plastic case for the ArduCAM CC3200 Uno from ArduCAM. This case will protect your alarm system and at the same time allow you access to the pins on the board as well as the camera interface, power connection, and usb connection. A picture of the case is shown in Figure 9-1.

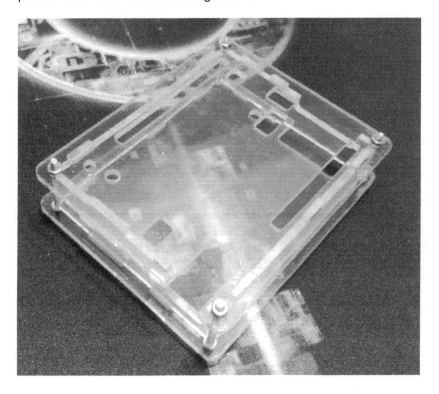

Figure 9-1. The ArduCAM CC3200 Uno case

Putting the Case Together

The case for the ArduCAM CC3200 Uno must be assembled. You can start by laying out the bottom and side portions that form the case as shown in Figure 9-2.

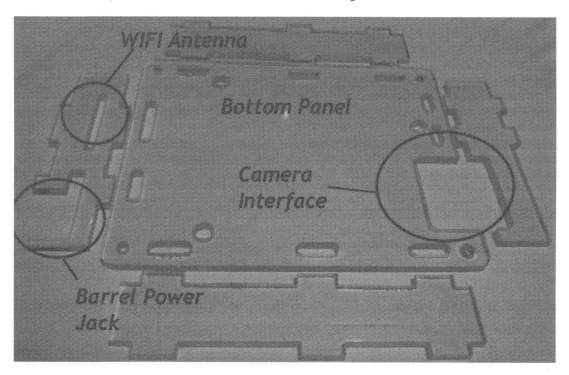

Figure 9-2. The bottom panel and side pieces of the case

The case also comes with the screws and bolts needed to attach the top panel of the case to the bottom panel of the case. You should also have some extended jumpers such as the one shown in Figure 9-3.

Figure 9-3. Extended jumpers

One important thing to note is that the wifi antenna attached to the CC3200 chip must go through a slot in the rear panel of the case as shown in Figure 9-4. There is also a plastic screw and nut included that can be used if needed to secure the board to the case through one of the 3 holes on the board and on the bottom panel.

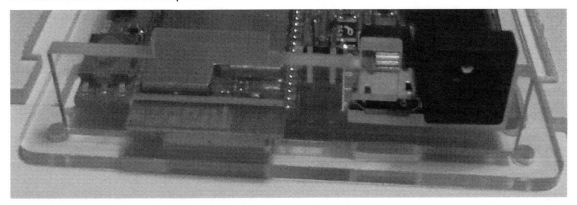

Figure 9-4. The wifi communications antenna must fit through the slot

Once you get the wifi antenna through the slot attach the other side panels onto the bottom panel of the case such as shown in Figure 9-5.

Figure 9-5. The ArduCAM CC3200 Uno inside the case without the top

Next, you need to attach the top panel to the case and then use the included screws and nuts to secure the top panel to the bottom panel as shown in Figure 9-6.

Figure 9-6. The ArduCAM CC3200 Uno with case fully assembled

The bottom side of the fully assembled case is shown in Figure 9-7.

Figure 9-7. The bottom of the ArduCAM CC3200 Uno inside the case

The top view of the final assembled case is shown in Figure 9-8.

Figure 9-8. The top of the ArduCAM CC3200 Uno case

Barrel Jack Power Input

The power input to the CC3200 device's power barrel jack must be in the range of 7 to 12 volts according to the official documentation. You will need either an AC adapter or a battery to power the CC3200 device through the jack. See Figure 9-9.

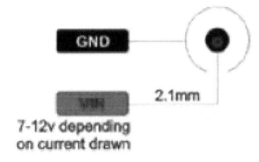

Figure 9-9. The power input voltage

Portable Power Supply

The document SWAS032F from Texas Instruments details the typical current usage of the CC3200 device when transmitting at full power as 278 mA. See Figure 9-10.

4.9 Current Consumption

T_A = +25°C, V_{BAT} = 3.6 V

PARAMETER			TEST CONDITIONS[1] [2]		MIN	TYP	MAX	UNIT
MCU ACTIVE	NWP ACTIVE	TX	1 DSSS	TX power level = 0		278		mA
				TX power level = 4		194		
			6 OFDM	TX power level = 0		254		
				TX power level = 4		185		
			54 OFDM	TX power level = 0		229		
				TX power level = 4		166		
		RX	1 DSSS			59		
			54 OFDM			59		
	NWP idle connected[3]					15.3		

Figure 9-10. CC3200 current specifications

A D size battery is 1.5 volts and has typical current rating of 12000-18000 mAh (milli-amphere hours). This means that the average D size battery can output 12000 to 18000 milli-amperes for one hour before being completely discharged. To operate the ArduCAM CC3200 Uno device I recommend you use 6 D size batteries which gives you a total of 9 volts. To determine the approximate number of hours you can operate the ArduCAM CC3200 Uno you would divide 278 into 12000 to get 43 hours of operation.

A D cell holder is shown in Figure 9-11 and is available for purchase in stores such as Amazon.com. Also you will need the right kind of connectors to connect the battery holder to the CC3200 device. These connectors can also be found on Amazon or Ebay for purchase.

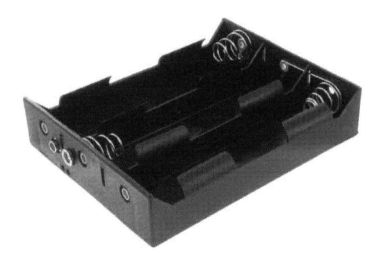

Figure 9-11. A D battery holder that holds 6 batteries

Deployment Ideas for Your New GotchaCAM Security and Surveillance System

This section discusses some ideas on how to deploy your new GotchaCAM security and surveillance system.

- OfficeCAM - Set up the surveillance system to find out who is "borrowing" your stuff at the office. Does your jar of candy on your desk seem to empty out faster than it normally does? Are you missing spare change from your desk drawer at work? Set up the GotchaCAM to catch the thief.

- RoommateCAM - Are you missing things from the room you are renting in a house full of other people you don't know? Hide the GotchCAM so that you can capture the thief.

- KidCAM - Check to see what your kids are doing while you are away from home.

- GrannyCAM – Monitor a parent or grand parent that resides in a nursing home or other managed care facility.

- RefrigeratorCAM – Prevent late night snacking by a family who is trying to loose weight. Place the GotchaCAM in front of the refrigerator to generate real time alerts whenever anyone tries to open the refrigerator door.

- RentalHouseCAM – Monitor an unoccupied rental home or apartment you own for intruders. Prevent squatters that try to take ownership of your home or apartment by moving in.

- NannyCAM – Monitor the baby sitter.

- MaidCAM – Monitor and track the maid or janitor that you hire to clean your home.

- TravelCAM – Monitor your hotel or motel room for intruders and receive real time notifications to your main cell phone.

- ApartmentCAM – Monitor your apartment for intruders while you are away at work and have real time notifications sent to your main cell phone.

- VacationHouseCAM – Monitor your empty vacation home for intruders while you are away.

- MainHouseCAM – Monitor you primary residence for intruders while you at work.

- TravelCAM – Monitor your hotel or motel room for unauthorized entry and capture a photo of the intruder.

- GhostCAM – Are you a professional or amateur ghost hunter and are not catching any ghosts on film? Well, use the GotchaCAM to capture these ghosts and to alert you in real time when the ghosts DO show up.